SpringerBriefs in Finance

For further volumes:
http://www.springer.com/series/10282

Pengcheng Song

Private Placement of Public Equity in China

Springer

Pengcheng Song
Department of Research and Development
China Huarong Asset Management Co., Ltd
and School of Finance
Renmin University of China
Beijing
China

ISSN 2193-1720 ISSN 2193-1739 (electronic)
ISBN 978-3-642-55092-8 ISBN 978-3-642-55093-5 (eBook)
DOI 10.1007/978-3-642-55093-5
Springer Heidelberg New York Dordrecht London

Library of Congress Control Number: 2014937265

Printed on acid-free paper

Springer is part of Springer Science+Business Media (www.springer.com)

To Baolian

Acknowledgments

This piece of research was conducted mostly when I was a Ph.D. student at School of Economics and Finance, University of Hong Kong. The draft has also been improved since I started to work as a fellow in the post-doctoral program co-sponsored by China Huarong Asset Management Co., Ltd and School of Finance, Renmin University of China. I would like to thank Editor Emmi Yang at Springer for her support during the whole publishing cycle.

I am still in search of a word that goes beyond thanks to recognize Dr. Xiaohui Gao, my supervisor, for her generous encouragement and support in my Ph.D. study. I wish to thank my fellow classmates, especially Dr. Zhiguo Wu and his wife Yandan Zhu, Dr. Qin Yang and Yong Wei and his wife Jialing Huang for the insights and fun generated through our friendship. Warm thoughts also go to the Guzy couple D. James Guzy, Jr. and Melissa C. Guzy, Nancy M. K. Li and Ye Xuan, who all offered invaluable help to me when I met a critical problem during the research.

Lastly, I reserve my special thanks for my grandparents, my parents Kunzhong Song and Tongying Zhao, my girlfriend Baolian Mao, and my younger brother Wanli Song, who have supported me with their love, patience and tolerance throughout.

Contents

Figures

Tables

Abstract

Private placement of public equity is much more popular than SEO and rights offering in China's equity refinancing practice, but has been scarcely studied. By retrieving entries from financial data vendor Wind and collecting relevant data from reading statements of private placements, I build a proprietary database and study five aspects of private placement in China.

First, I study which listed firms are more likely to choose private placement over SEO in refinancing. Firms whose controlling shareholder is state-owned and who want to establish business connections with potential investors are the most likely to conduct private placement. Secondly, I look into the controlling shareholder's decision whether to purchase privately placed shares or not. The controlling shareholder does not care about holdings dilution caused by not participating in a private placement. No matter how severe information asymmetry is on the issuer's true value, there are always institutional investors contributing capital to it, so its largest shareholder does not have to participate in the offering for the sake of solving under-investment problem. Thirdly, I investigate how the offer discount is determined. China's private placements are sold to investors at an average discount of 24.83 %. Such discount does not reflect the largest shareholder or institutional investors' increased monitoring efforts after the placement. There is also no consistent evidence that information costs explain the discount. In private placements where the largest shareholder buys shares, however, the discount is as high as 43.16 %. Fourthly, I calculate the announcement period abnormal return of private placements. The abnormal return is significantly positive. Again, increased monitoring from the largest shareholder or big institutional investors does not explain the positivity. There is mixed evidence whether the reduction of information asymmetry causes positive announcement-period abnormal return, and inadequate evidence whether more credible information leads to higher market reaction. Fifthly, but not finally, I document positive long-run abnormal return of private offerings, evidence supportive of the under-reaction hypothesis.

All the adventure indicates that the largest shareholder does not deserve the excess discount in the placement. The largest shareholder can ask for a lower price than institutional investors' for a longer locking period of private shares, but it does not, showing that liquidity is not its concern. It does not have to contribute capital to the issuer for under-subscription of shares, because no matter how uncertain firm value is, institutional investors are willing to dedicate enough proceeds.

Thus, information asymmetry is not a problem for the largest shareholder either. Positive long-run abnormal return also fails to explain the excess discount. I argue that the largest shareholder tunnels by excess discount, rational of itself but harmful to other shareholders.

Chapter 1
Introduction

Abstract This is the introductory chapter of the book. The main reason I am motivated to study private placement in China is that it is the most popular equity refinancing method but has not been thoroughly studied. In this chapter, I first show the popularity of private placement in China relative to SEO and rights offering. Then I introduce main findings and contribution of the study.

Keywords Private placement • PIPE • Discount • Abnormal return • Market reaction • Tunneling

1.1 Motivation: Private Placement in China and Its Popularity

Different from SEOs (seasoned equity offerings) in which shares of the issuing firm are offered to the public and rights offerings in which shares are offered to existing shareholders, in private placements of public equity shares are sold to existing blockholders and institutional investors[1] without public participation. In China where a listed firm usually has a largest shareholder/controlling shareholder, a private placement is reduced to an offering to the largest shareholder and institutional investors.

Despite private placement's popularity as a method of refinancing, Hertzel and Smith (1993)'s assertion that it is among the least studied subjects in equity offering still holds true today. Anderson et al. (2006) document the popularity of private placements against other means of seasoned offerings in New Zealand. The case is more striking in China. It is not until May 2006, when CSRC (China Securities Regulation Committee) published *Regulatory Measures of Securities Issuance for Listed Companies,* did private placements pass the stage of being experimental and scarce. For more than 5 years since then, private placements have been surging. Not

[1] In this study, I treat high-net-worth investors as institutional investors.

P. Song, *Private Placement of Public Equity in China*, SpringerBriefs in Finance,
DOI: 10.1007/978-3-642-55093-5_1, © The Author(s) 2014

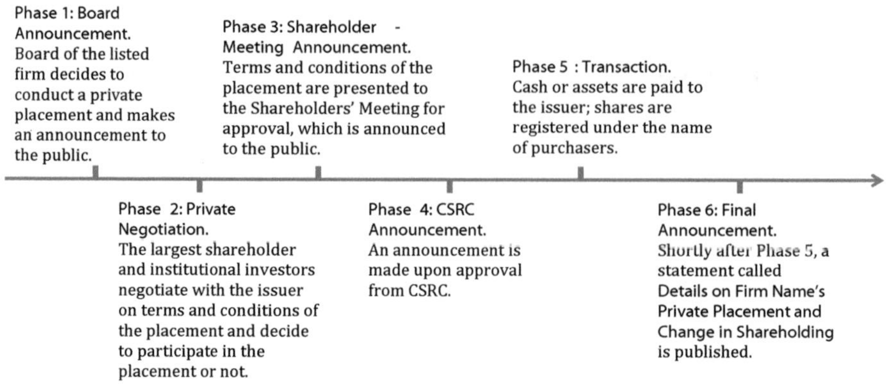

Fig. 1.1 Timeline of a private placement in China's Stock Market. This figure shows the process a private placement is carried out in China. In Phase 1, a statement endorsed by the issuer's board members is released to the public, informing nothing but that the issuer is brooding a private placement. In Phase 2, potential investors including large shareholders of the issuer and institutional investors privately negotiate on terms of the private placement. These terms include proceeds to raise, offering price and number of shares to be allotted to each participating investor. In Phase 3, a statement endorsed by the shareholders' meeting is released to the public, informing nothing but that shareholders have approved terms of the offering. In Phase 4, a statement containing CSRC's approval of the private offering is released. Again, no more information on the offering is released. Relevant parties of the offering settle the transaction in Phase 5, immediately after which is Phase 6 when, finally, details of the private placement are released to the public

only does the absolute number of private placements increase at a high rate yearly, this type of seasoned offering also surpasses its public counterparts SEO and rights offering in proceeds raised.[2] Again, despite its importance, there has been no systemic study making use of private placement data in China.

Figure 1.1 shows the timeline of a private placement in China, as the same in most other countries.

Three regulatory features of private placements in China are worth mentioning. Firstly, CSRC requires that the offering price should not be lower than 90 % of the stock's average price for the 20 days prior to board announcement. The literature has documented offering discount in private placements: purchasers enjoy a discount to prevailing market price. Existence of a price floor in China allows me to calculate the premium of offering price to the price floor, thus examine investors' cost from another perspective. Secondly, a locking period of 12 months for institutional investors and that of 36 months for the controlling shareholder are imposed. As a result, investors face different restriction periods after the placement. The largest shareholder with a longer locking period can ask for a lower offering price/higher offering discount if it considers illiquidity a substantial problem. Thirdly, shares can be offered to different investors at different prices. However, as will be

[2] I provide detailed comparisons among private placement, SEO and rights offering in Chap. 3.

shown in Chap. 4, I do not observe different offering prices for any single private placement: the largest shareholder is not concerned about restrictions on resale and glad to have the same offering price with institutional investors.

While there are cross-country differences in regulating private placements, there is only one outstanding: shares cannot be sold to large shareholders in Singapore. This implies that in countries rather than Singapore, the controlling shareholder who by definition is influential on firm decisions, can play an important if not central role in determining the terms of a private placement. The largest shareholder, being self-interested and rational, can enjoy private benefits of control and tunnel wealth from other shareholders to itself by at least three ways. Firstly, if the largest shareholder would like to increase its stake, it can initiate a private placement and inject cash or assets into the firm, even if the firm is in no need of extra capital at all. Secondly, a related party of the largest shareholder can inject cash/assets into the firm and profit from the firm's growth prospects while the firm already has adequate capital. Thirdly, even if the firm does need extra capital, the largest shareholder can ask for as many shares as possible in return for a given amount of cash/assets, or put in another way, ask for an unfairly high discount it does not deserve. A large part of this study is to determine economic consequences of such placements in which the controlling shareholder participates, either alone or joined by institutional investors.

1.2 Findings on Offering Discount

In this study, I find an offering discount of averagely 24.83 % for China's private placements. SEC (1971) of the US documents that in the US, issuing price is on average 30 % lower than the market price for private placements. Ensuing empirical studies with US data document discounts of 11.3–20 % (Wruck 1989; Hertzel and Smith 1993; Hertzel et al. 2002). Discounts also apply to cases of Korea (Kang 1990), Japan (Kato and Schallheim 1993), and New Zealand (Anderson 2006). In Singapore, however, Tan et al. (2002) find most private placed shares are sold at a premium.

The *Monitoring Hypothesis* that purports investors should enjoy a discount for their increased monitoring efforts after a private placement cannot explain the discount in China. My regressions show that, neither the controlling shareholder nor institutional investors ask for compensation to more monitoring efforts. I do find evidence that the discount can partially be explained by information costs that investors incur in determining the issuer's true value, thus the *Information Cost Hypothesis* holds in China.

The average discount of private placements in which the controlling shareholder of the issuer participates, joined or not joined by institutional investors, is higher by 43.61 % than that of private placements in which shares are only sold to institutional investors (at an average discount of 8.50 %). This is evidence supporting the *Tunneling Hypothesis* that says the controlling shareholder takes private placement as a chance to buy as many shares and dilute as much the holdings of other shareholders as possible with a given amount of capital.

The controlling shareholder can defend its extra discount with three reasons. First, it faces a longer locking period after placement than institutional investors. Second, institutional investors are not willing to purchase enough shares, so the controlling shareholder has to contribute capital to the issuer. Third, the issuing firm's intrinsic value is lower than market value in the long run, so the controlling shareholder deserves a discount to compensate for future loss. I have refuted the first reason by showing that in private placements where the controlling shareholder and institutional investors are both purchasers, the former does not ask for a lower price than the latter to compensate longer restriction period. I refute the second reason by my study in Chap. 3 and show that there are always institutional investors willing to contribute adequate capital to the issuer. That is to say, no matter how uncertain the issuing firm's value is, the controlling shareholder never has to worry about undersubscription. There is no gap between proceeds the issuer wants to raise and contributions institutional investors would like to make for the controlling shareholder to fill. Finally, I invalidate the third reason by Chap. 6, which shows that stocks of private placement firms exhibit positive long-run abnormal returns. My investigations put together serve to prove that the largest shareholder does not deserve an excess discount: the largest shareholder uses private placement as a channel of tunneling wealth from other shareholders to itself.

1.3 Findings on Announcement Effect

I document positive abnormal announcement-period returns for private placements in China: 4.30 % around board announcement and 2.23 % around final announcement. This is in line with Wruck (1989) who documents a 4.5 % average abnormal return on the announcement of private placements and Hertzel and Smith (1993) who find a smaller but still positive effect of 1.72 % for the case of US. Such positive announcement effects are also found in Japan (Kato and Schallheim 1993) and Hong Kong (Wu et al. 2005).[3] In addition, Janney and Folta (2003) document announcement effects of the same direction for a sample of the Biotechnology Industry. Consistency in announcement effects in private placements across countries and industries are different from mixed results in SEOs and rights issues.[4]

[3] In the case of Singapore, although Tan et al. (2002) document positive abnormal returns for the announcement period using a 1987–1996 sample, Chen et al. (2003) find significant negative announcement effect. I will discuss more in the literature review of Chap. 2.

[4] Studies on seasoned public offering in the US have documented unanimously negative abnormal returns for the announcement period (Smith 1977; Myers and Majluf 1984; Masulis and Korwar 1986; Eckbo and Masulis 1992). The sign of announcement effect for rights issues, however, is ambiguous. Smith (1977) documents insignificant abnormal returns in US rights issues, while Eckbo and Masulis (1992) point out that right issues in the US are followed by significant negative abnormal returns upon announcement. For Korea, Kang (1990) shows that there is positive abnormal announcement-period return. Ariff and Finn (1989) also find the same positive effect in Singapore. Australia and New Zealand (Marsden 2000), on the contrary, experience negative abnormal announcement-period returns.

As in the case of explaining discounts, I find no evidence that the market reacts to any change of ownership, or the increase in monitoring efforts as purported by some researchers to result from a more concentrated ownership structure; therefore I dismiss the *Monitoring Effect* around announcement period. Neither does my evidence support the *Signaling Effect*. On the one hand, I find mixed evidence on whether the market reacts positively to reduction of information asymmetry due to information disclosed by private placement announcements. On the other hand, my proposition that more credible information leads to higher market reaction is not supported either.

1.4 Findings on Long-Term Performance

I document positive long-term abnormal stock returns for private placements in China using both the BHAR approach and the calendar-time portfolio approach. Considering positive announcement-period abnormal returns, I propose that the *Under-reaction Hypothesis* holds. The market does not react fully to information released around announcement, but continue to adjust upwards into the future. This is not only inconsistent with Spiess and Affleck-Graves (1995) and Loughran and Ritter (1997) who find that in SEOs, the issuer experiences abnormally low return over the 5 years after announcement, but also not in line with Hertzel et al. (2002) that document negative long-run performance of as much as −23.8 %. Krishnamurthy et al. (2005), Barclay et al. (2007) and Chou et al. (2009) also document long-term abnormally low returns in general, but find some of their subsamples experience positive long-term performance.

I divide my sample in order to find if long-run performance differs across subsamples. Unfortunately, as Hertzel et al. (2002) fail for the US case, there seems to be no independent variable that helps explain positive long-run returns.

1.5 Contribution of the Study

This study is the first to provide solid evidence that tunneling is present in private placements. This contribution is in striking contrast to the extant literature that appears to be ignoring the prevalence of concentrated ownership structures around the globe. I add to the literature both on private placement of public equity and on private benefits of control of which tunneling is an important form.

I design new variables to test hypotheses. When measuring ownership concentration, extant studies do not differentiate holdings of different shareholders. In this book, I make a distinction between ownership of the controlling shareholder and that of institutional investors. Thus, instead of claiming ambiguously that a more concentrated ownership does not help explain discount/market reaction, I am able to specify that increased holdings of neither the controlling shareholder nor institutional investors have explanatory power. This is an addition to the literature on behaviors of the controlling shareholder and institutional investors. I also construct more variables indicating information asymmetry than used in the existing literature. For example, the number of institutional investors participating in a private placement is employed to proxy how credible the signal on firm value is. Moreover, the number of years that an issuer has been listed is used to measure the level of information asymmetry on the issuer.

This book proceeds as follows. In Chap. 2 I provide a literature review firstly on private benefits of control (including tunneling) that are inherent in block-holding, and then on three aspects of private placements of equity: discount determination, announcement effect, and long-term performance. In Chap. 3 I study a listed firm's choice between private placement and SEO when in need of refinancing and the largest shareholder's choice of whether to participate in the private placement or not. Chaps. 4, 5 and 6 deal with discount determination, announcement-period abnormal return and long-run abnormal return respectively. Chapter 7 concludes the book.

References

Anderson HD (2006) Discounted private placements in New Zealand: exploitation or fair compensation. Working Paper, Massey University

Anderson HD, Rose LC, Cahan SF (2006) Differential shareholder wealth and volume effects surrounding private equity placements in New Zealand. Pac Basin Finan J 14:367–395

Ariff M, Finn FJ (1989) Announcement effects and market efficiency in a thin market: an empirical application to the Singapore equity market. Asia Pac J Manage 6:243–265

Barclay MJ, Holderness CG, Sheehan DP (2007) Private placements and managerial entrenchment. J Corp Finan 13:461–484

Chen S-S, Ho KW, Lee C-F, Yeo GHH (2003) Wealth effects of private equity placements: evidence from Singapore. Finan Rev 37:165–183

Chou D-W, Gombola M, Liu F-Y (2009) Long-run underperformance following private equity placements: The role of growth opportunities. Q Rev Econ Finan 49:1113–1128

Eckbo BE, Masulis RW (1992) Adverse selection and the rights offer paradox. J Financ Econ 32:293–332

Hertzel M, Smith RL (1993) Market discounts and shareholder gains for placing equity privately. J Finan 48:459–485

Hertzel M, Lemmon M, Linck JS, Rees L (2002) Long-run performance following private placements of equity. J Finan 57:2595–2617

Janney JJ, Folta TB (2003) The impact of timing and other signal characteristics on returns to private equity placements: the case of Biotechnology. J Bus Ventur 18:361–380

Kang H (1990) Effects of seasoned equity offerings in Korea on shareholder's wealth. In: Rhee S, Chang R (ed) Pacific-Basin Capital Markets Research, North-Holland

Kato K, Schallheim JS (1993) Private equity financings in Japan and corporate grouping (keiretsu). Pac Basin Finan J 1:287–307

Krishnamurthy S, Spindt P, Subramaniam V, Woidtke Tracie (2005) Does investor identity matter in equity issues? Evidence from private placements. J Finan Intermediation 14:210–238

Loughran T, Ritter J (1997) The operating performance of firms conducting seasoned equity offerings. J Finan 52:1823–1850

Marsden A (2000) Shareholder wealth effects of rights issues: evidence from the New Zealand capital market. Pac Bas Finan J 8:419–442

Masulis RW, Korwar AN (1986) Seasoned equity offerings: an empirical investigation. J Financ Econ 15:91–118

Myers S, Majluf NS (1984) Corporate financing and investment decisions when firms have information that investors do not have. J Finan Econ 13:187–221

Securities and Exchange Commission (1971) Institutional investor study report of the Securities and Exchange Commission. U.S. Government Printing Office, Washington, D.C.

Smith CW (1977) Alternative methods for raising capital: Rights versus underwritten offerings. J Financ Econ 5:273–307

Spiess DK, Affleck-Graves J (1995) Underperformance in long-run stock returns following seasoned equity offerings. J Finan Econ 38:243–267

Tan RSK, Chng PL, Tong YH (2002) Private placements and rights issues in Singapore. Pac Basin Fin J 10:29–54

Wruck KH (1989) Equity ownership concentration and firm value: evidence from private equity financings. J Financ Econ 23:3–28

Wu X, Wang Z, Yao J (2005) Understanding the positive announcement effects of private equity placements: new insights from Hong Kong data. Rev Finan 9:385–414

Chapter 2
Literature Review

Abstract In this chapter, I summarize and comment on the literature related to private placement. I start from reviewing studies on private benefits of control and tunneling. Then I focus on private placement and summarize the literature along four lines: the choice among equity refinancing methods, discount determination, announcement effect, and long-run performance. Finally I discuss the absence of treatment of tunneling in the private placement literature.

Keywords Private placement • PIPE • Discount • Abnormal return • Market reaction • Tunneling

Extant studies on private placements focus on four aspects. The first is characteristics of private shares issuers, or why a firm conducts a private equity offering instead of a public one such as SEO or rights offering. The second and the third are factors that determine offering discount and announcement-period abnormal return respectively. The fourth is the long-run stock price behavior and operating performance of the issuer.

There is almost no discussion on whether tunneling is present in private placements in the existing literature, although researchers have been documenting that firms issuing private shares are of high ownership concentration, namely the existence of influential large shareholders.[1] The controlling shareholder may dilute holdings of other shareholders by offering private shares to itself, even if the firm is not in need of refinancing. Even if the firm does need additional funding, the controlling shareholder may arbitrarily lower the offering price and purchase as many shares as possible for a given amount of capital. Tunneling is especially important for a study related to corporate governance in China. Cheung et al. (2006) find that in Hong Kong's stock market, connected-party transaction as a form of tunneling is more prevalent in listed companies whose ultimate controller can be traced back to Mainland China. My study in part is an extension of the literature on private

[1] It's not unfair to say that ownership structure is concentrated in most economies of the world.

P. Song, *Private Placement of Public Equity in China*, SpringerBriefs in Finance,
DOI: 10.1007/978-3-642-55093-5_2, © The Author(s) 2014

benefits of control and tunneling; therefore I review literature on large-percentage shareholding (and private benefits of control and tunneling that are inherent therein) before proceeding to literature on private placements of equity.

2.1 Private Benefits of Control and Tunneling

Berle and Means (1932) make great contribution to our understanding of the principal-agent problem between shareholders and firm management. The other form of agency problem, which results from interest conflicts between large shareholders and other shareholders,[2] did not catch economists' attention until decades later. To identify the ultimate shareholder of large corporations in 27 economies around the globe, La Porta et al. (1999) find few of these firms featured by diffused ownership. They suggest, "The principal agent problem in large corporations around the world is that restricting expropriation of minority shareholders by the controlling shareholders, rather than of restricting empire building by professional managers unaccountable to shareholders".

Large shareholding is generally motivated by shared benefits of control and private benefits of control. Jensen and Meckling (1976) and Shleifer and Vishny (1986) argue that the existence of block-holders helps mitigate the agency problem between shareholders and firm management, providing non-exclusive benefits to all shareholders. An incentive problem naturally arises: How can the block-holder be adequately motivated to monitor the management if resulting benefits are to be shared with minor shareholders, a phenomenon called free-riding in incentive theory. Barclay and Holderness (1989) provide the first evidence that there are exclusive benefits to block-holders. They find blocks of shares are traded at an average of 20 % premium to prevailing market price. The premium reflects private benefits of control and is confirmed by Mikkelson and Regassa (2000), Nicodano and Sembenelli (2004) and Dyck and Zingales (2002).[3]

---

[2] In 1983, a special issue of Journal of Financial Economics was dedicated to the principal-agent problem between diffused shareholders and firm management. 5 years later, in 1988, another special issue of the same journal focused on the agency problem between large-percentage shareholders and small shareholders.

[3] Nicodano and Sembenelli (2004) document even larger premium of block trading in Italy than in the US and purport that the less restraining the legal system is, the more private benefits of control. Dyck and Zingales (2002) use the same method of measuring premium in block trading and document that the average value of control is 14 % across 39 countries of concern. Researchers have also attempted to determine private benefits of control via another method making use of the fact that some stocks are endowed with voting rights while some are not. Chung and Kim (1999) find that private benefits of control in Korea, measured by the premium enjoyed by the voting stock over the non-voting stock, is about 10 % of equity value. According to Claessens et al. (2002), private benefits of control also exist as a result of the discrepancy between cash flow rights and control rights of the controlling shareholder.

Private benefits of control to the controlling shareholder are not necessarily harmful to non-controlling shareholders.[4] Johnson et al. (2000) coin the term *tunneling* as the part of private benefits of control that is harmful to non-controlling shareholders. As they put, tunneling can take the form of related-party transactions including outright theft, pricing advantage in asset transfers, loan guarantee and so on, or the form of financial transactions such as intentionally diluting small shareholders' holdings and insider trading. Tunneling through related-party transaction has been extensively studied since Johnson et al. (2000). Baek et al. (2006) find evidence of tunneling in Korean business groups as Cheung et al. (2006) do for Hong Kong. In the case of China, Jian and Wong (2003) find that business groups as controlling shareholders tunnel more than holdings companies.

Some works propose that it is unfair to always blame the controlling shareholder for tunneling: The controlling shareholder can also prop the firm in financial distress. Bai et al. (2004) argue that entities with strong financial condition are willing to compete for the position of controlling shareholder of a STed[5] firm and help it regain financial strength. Peng et al. (2011) find that in China, when a firm is financially healthy, connected-party transactions are used to tunnel while if the firm is in trouble, such transactions are used to prop. However, authors of both studies concede that propping is just a cost for benefits of tunneling in the future.

2.2 The Choice Among Equity Refinancing Methods

A listed firm can issue additional shares privately or publicly, and to existing or new shareholders. Generally, the firm has three options of increasing cost if it decides not to pursue a private placement: Non-underwritten rights offering, underwritten rights offering and bookbuilt offering in which underwriters are employed to create prospectus and market shares.[6] In a rights offering, the firm sells shares to existing shareholders on a pro rata basis. If a substantial number of shareholders do not purchase new shares allotted to them, the firm is not able to raise the amount of capital as planned. In a non-underwritten rights offering, this is called the *lack of guarantee* problem. In an underwritten rights offering, however, the underwriter agrees to buy all shares not wanted by existing shareholders. Such a guarantee comes at the expense of underwriting fees. In bookbuilt offerings, shares are offered to all investors, although incumbent shareholders enjoy priority in allotment if shares are oversubscribed.

---

[4] For example, the controlling shareholder may derive pleasure and a sense of privilege out of its control position. This does no harm to other shareholders.

[5] ST is the abbreviation of Special Treatment. A listed firm in China's Shanghai and Shenzhen stock markets is said to be under Special Treatment if it shows negative financial abnormality. ST can be used as a verb in the same manner. Bai et al. (2004) provide a detailed description of ST.

[6] Gao (2008) provides an excellent investigation into more recent developments, such as accelerated offering, in seasoned equity offering. For the purpose of this study, I stop short of accelerated offerings.

A vast amount of literature are dedicated to explain the so called *Equity Refinancing Paradox*, which can be phrased in two parts: Why would a firm hire underwriters to do rights offering or bookbuilt offering while it can by itself do a non-underwritten rights offering for free; and why would a firm hire the underwriter for bookbuilt offering while the underwriting fee for rights offering is lower. Smith (1977) is the first to document the first part of *Equity Refinancing Paradox*: Although the cost of non-underwritten rights issue is substantially lower than public offering that is underwritten by default, 90 % of US firms employ the latter method for equity refinancing. Booth and Smith (1986) theorize that underwriters play a role of certification in equity offerings. Hansen (1998) addresses the second part of *Equity Refinancing Paradox* and proposes that underwritten rights offerings, although requiring lower underwriting fees, are associated with substantial transaction costs that do not happen to bookbuilt offerings.

Eckbo and Masulis (1992) posit that the choice of equity-refinancing method is dependent on the degree of information asymmetry between firm insiders and the public, characteristics of shareholders and the cost of direct financing. They argue that underwriting by investment banks and active subscription by existing shareholders are the main means of solving information asymmetry and avoiding wealth transfer from existing shareholders to potential shareholders. To maximize firm value in the presence of information asymmetry, firm management has to employ equity-refinancing methods of certain costs, which are costs of adverse selection due to information asymmetry.

Information asymmetry is also employed to explain why firms choose private placement instead of seasoned public offering. Using a sample of listed US high-technology firms, Wu (2004) finds the value of a firm conducting private placement is more uncertain than that of a bookbuilt-offering firm. Cronqvist and Nisson (2005) make a comparison between firms conducting private placements and rights offerings in Sweden and show that a typical firm resorts to non-underwritten rights offering, underwritten rights offering and finally private placement in order as the degree of information asymmetry on firm value goes higher. Marciukaityte et al. (2005) study a sample of 513 US firms that undertook private equity placement between 1979 and 1996 and find a large percentage of them to be young, small, and high-R&D-expenditure firms whose value is hard to evaluate. This lends strong support to the information-asymmetry explanation of why firms choose private placements.

Besides information asymmetry, the literature has also examined the choice of private versus public offering from the angle of ownership structure. According to Shleifer and Vishny (1986), private placements that result in a more concentrated ownership will lead to more monitoring on management and increase firm value. Moreover, since private placed shares are restricted from resale for a certain period after the placement, outside investors are not able to 'vote by feet' but are incentivized to monitor firm management (Kahn and Winton 1998). Wruck (1989) is the first to explain the choice of private placement by higher ownership concentration. Hertzel and Smith (1993) support such an explanation, but subsequent studies pose serious challenge to it. Wu (2004) find that investors of privately placed shares are no more active in monitoring than those of public offerings. What's more, Cronqvist and Nisson (2005) find that controlling shareholders in Sweden prefer rights offering to private placement because the former does not induce any decrease in their control rights or increase in outsider monitoring. They also find that even if the controlling shareholder chooses private placement, it not infrequently issues shares to itself so as to strengthen entrenchment and evade more monitoring from outside investors. Therefore, it seems that private placements are chosen over public offerings mainly due to information asymmetry, but not more monitoring.

Cronqvist and Nisson (2005) also find firms employ private placements to establish business relations with potential industrial partners. By privately issuing shares to firm B whose supplier is firm A, firm A can align B's interest with its own and get rid of the hold-up problem, a type of moral hazard.

In sum, extant studies on the choice of private placement against public offering stress the role of information asymmetry and the need to form business alliance, but challenge the ownership structure perspective.

2.3 Discount Determination

Since privately placed shares are generally restricted from resale for a certain period,[7] it is easy to understand, according to Silber (1992), that lack of liquidity can explain part of the discount. There are three more hypotheses that have been proposed to explain the discount.

Monitoring Hypothesis. It claims the discount is what purchasers of privately placed shares are paid for shared benefits of control from higher ownership concentration after the private placement.

The pioneer work of Wruck (1989) observes an increase of share ownership from 31 to 37 % by managers, directors and the controlling shareholder.[8] Wruck thus hypothesizes that the discount serves as compensation to participating investors for increased monitoring efforts on the management team after a private sale of shares. In other words, participants in the private placement are awarded a discount for reducing the principal-agent problem between shareholders and the management. Using data of private placements in Hong Kong, Wu et al. (2005) find that higher ownership concentration does lead to better use of investment opportunities.

There are two problems with the *Monitoring Hypothesis*. The first is its underlying assumption that shared benefits of control surpass private benefits of control. Cronqvist and Nisson (2005) pose a challenge by showing that firms controlled by families are prone to use private offering to avoid monitoring. This implies that for participating investors, private offering of equity may be a channel of strengthening private benefits of control, but not sharing benefits with other shareholders. Barclay et al. (2007) and Wu (2004)'s studies on

---

[7] There is no such restriction in New Zealand.

[8] Wruck (1989) treats 5 % as the threshold between substantial and non-substantial shareholders, i.e., if a shareholder owns more than 5 % of a firm, then it is counted in when calculating the ownership concentration measure.

US firms reveal that participants of private placements do not necessarily provide better monitoring. The other problem with this hypothesis is it does not explain the discount of private placements after which ownership concentration does not increase. Hertzel and Smith (1993) propose the *Information Cost Hypothesis* as part of the solution to this problem.

Information Cost Hypothesis. This hypothesis says that investors buy private placed shares at a discount because they need to be compensated for costs induced in the process of making investment decisions. Such investment-decision process involves studying the firm's ability to grow to a larger size, to generate a higher return with the current asset size, or to take advantage of investment opportunities.

Hertzel and Smith (1993) extend Myers and Majluf (1984)'s model and propose that the fact firm management chooses private placement and investors are willing to purchase shares signals to the market that the firm is undervalued. Using a different sample set of the US from that of Wruck's (1989), Hertzel and Smith (1993) on the one hand supports the *Monitoring Hypothesis*, and on the other hand argues that the discount can be explained to a larger extent by information cost. Firms in their sample are smaller than these in Wruck (1989), so their finding that *Monitoring Hypothesis* is of secondary importance is consistent with Morck et al. (1988) that ownership structure is more important for large firms. Hertzel and Smith (1993) do not distinguish growth in firm size (scale) and growth upon current size (productivity). Wu et al. (2005) find that in Hong Kong information cost is mainly induced to verify the issuer's potential to grow to a larger size, but not growth per se.

The *Information Cost Hypothesis* is unable to explain why the controlling shareholder who should know the true value of the firm for free is offered a discount. This is not the whole picture, however. Both the *Monitoring Hypothesis* and the *Information Cost Hypothesis* purport that after a private placement, non-participants are better off. They may benefit from a better-monitored management or harder working by the management to realize good investment opportunities. Barclay et al. (2007) propose the *Passive Investor Hypothesis* and prove empirically that private placement of equity may do non-participants no good.

Passive Investor Hypothesis. This hypothesis claims that in a private sale of equity, management of the issuer offers shares at a discount to passive investors[9] who will not interfere with firm management after the issue and facilitate management entrenchment. The discount is regarded as compensation to passive investors for keeping silent about firm management.

Dann and DeAngelo (1983) are the first to offer evidence on this hypothesis. They find that private placement is in the management's toolkit to defend potential takeovers. Barclay et al. (2007) study the long-term performance of firms that undertake private placements and find that passive investors won't have positive long-term abnormal returns unless they purchase shares at a big discount at the private placement. Given their finding that shareholders of the firm who do not

---

9 Barclay et al. (2007) define investors who do not reportedly interact with the issuer after a private placement as passive investors.

participate in the private offering experience long-term loss, they argue that the loss is due to management entrenchment facilitated by passive investors.

2.3.1 Announcement Effect

Positive abnormal return around the announcement period is widely documented in private placement literature. Researchers have proposed three effects to explain positive short-run market reaction.

Monitoring Effect. This is the sister version of *Monitoring Hypothesis* in explaining discount. Public investors react positively to the announcement of a private placement because they believe higher ownership concentration leads to more monitoring on the management. Wruck (1989) first proposes this effect, followed by Wu et al. (2005). Chen et al. (2003)'s study on private placements in Singapore is the only one to document negative announcement effect, but they argue, in favor of *Monitoring Effect*, that this is due to decrease in ownership concentration.[10]

More monitoring after the private placement may come not from the controlling shareholder, but new block-holders: The market may also react positively to the fact that among investors participating in the private placement, there are active ones who will interfere with the management and help increase firm value.[11] Wruck and Wu (2002) find that higher announcement effects follow private placements whose investors include these that are newly connected to the issuer. They argue that these newly acquainted investors will do a better monitoring job than familiar investors. Barclay et al. (2007) find that in the US the positive announcement effect is mainly driven by private placements offered to active investors.

Signaling Effect. As the sister version of *Information Cost Hypothesis* in explaining discount, this effect says the market believes a private placement signals that the issuing firm can grow to a larger size, gain higher earnings power with the current size, or make profitable uses of investment opportunities. Hertzel and Smith (1993) find the positive market reaction is mainly from the belief that an issuer can either grow larger or earn more without growth of asset size. Tan et al. (2002) argue that in Singapore the announcement effect is positively related to issue size that is an indicator of the issuer's investment opportunity. Wu et al. (2005) find in Hong Kong, positive market reaction of private placements can be partly attributed to the belief that the issuer has growth potentials. Anderson et al. (2006) point out that in New Zealand, the announcement-day effect of placements whose proceeds are used for capital expenditure or new projects is positive while that of placements whose proceeds are used for working capital or refinancing is negative or insignificant.

---

[10] In Singapore, privately placed shares are not allowed to be purchased by existing block-holders, so ownership concentration is destined to be lower after a private placement.

[11] This is different from *Monitoring Effect* in which monitoring is exerted by the controlling shareholder.

Janney and Folta (2006) show that in the Biotechnology Industry, the more renowned the investor is, the higher announcement effect following a private placement. Krishnamurthy et al. (2005) observe that the market reacts more favorably to private placements offered to affiliated investors that know better about firm value than those offered to unaffiliated investors.[12] Finally, Anderson et al. (2006) document premiums rather than discounts in private placements in New Zealand. They purport these premiums are credible signals showing the market that issuers are undervalued.

It's worth noting that in both effects mentioned above, the market does not necessarily only react to credible signals. The fact that ownership is more concentrated after a private placement does not necessarily mean firm value will increase. The fact that institutional investors have incurred costs in studying the firm's true value does not mean their judgment is right. The news that proceeds of the private issue will be used in making new investments does not credibly convey the idea that the issuer can make good uses of these investment opportunities.

Projection Effect. This effect says the more optimistic investors are at the time of private placement, the higher announcement-period abnormal return. The projection argument in Marciukaityte et al. (2005) says that investors are prone to forecast the performance of firms whose values are much uncertain on the basis of market condition: The more firms performing beyond investors' expectation now, the more optimistic investors are about uncertain firms' prospects. They use the number of beyond-expectation firms before a private placement as indicator of investor over-optimism and find that most of the firms in their sample are of uncertain firm values and that the more optimistic investors are, the higher the short-run market reaction to the issuer's stock.

There are two other perspectives that should be noted in any study on the announcement-period abnormal return of equity refinancing. The first is *Price Pressure Effect*, introduced simultaneously by Scholes (1972) and Kraus and Stoll (1972). Assuming that the demand curve for securities is downward sloping, this hypothesis claims an increase in the supply of a stock due to seasoned offering causes downside pressure on stock price. Anderson et al. (2006) do trace significant price pressure effect for private placements in New Zealand.[13] The second is *Wealth Transfer Effect* widely cited in the literature on M&A, managerial compensation, and dividend and share repurchase announcements [see, for example, DeFusco et al. (1990) and Handjinicolaou and Kalay (1984)]. In the case of equity refinancing, this hypothesis says that seasoned equity makes leverage of the issuer lower and that wealth is transferred from stockholders to bondholders. For private

---

[12] Krishnamurthy et al. (2005) define affiliated investors as officers, directors and affiliated institutions.

[13] Not all private placements in New Zealand are featured by a discount. In Anderson et al. (2006), downside price pressure only appears in these private placements in which shares are offered at a discount.

placement, however, no evidence supporting this hypothesis is found in either Singapore or New Zealand (Tan et al. 2002; Anderson et al. 2006).

2.4 Long-Run Performance

A vast amount of research focusing on the long horizon has shown that compared to control firms, firms that conduct seasoned public offerings perform worse, in both stock price and operating performance. For example, Spiess and Affleck-Graves (1995) not only document inferior operating performance of issuers, but also find stocks of such firms underperform stocks of non-issuing controls by as much as 31.2 % in a 5-year horizon. The same pattern is also documented in Loughran and Ritter (1997). At least for SEOs in the US, it is established that there are negative excess returns in both the short and long horizons.

Two hypotheses are proposed to coordinate the dual negativities. The first is *Under-reaction Hypothesis*. Assuming investors are conservative, this hypothesis posits that investors do not react fully to undesirable information released around the announcement period but only adjust gradually towards the long end. The second is *Over-optimism Hypothesis*. It says, for some reason, investors are over-optimistic when bad information is published but are able to make neutral judgments given enough time. Loughran and Ritter (1997) offer the first evidence for *Over-optimism Hypothesis*. They apply Kahneman and Tversky (1982)'s proposition that human beings give recent experience more weights than distant experience in making judgments and purport that investor over-optimism arises from enhanced firm financial performance immediately prior to the issue. They also develop the notion of 'window of opportunity' and argue that firm management is able to time the SEO at when investors are over-optimistic. Negativity of abnormal return in the short run and the same in the long run for SEOs become compatible under the *Over-optimism Hypothesis*.

Hertzel et al. (2002) and Chou et al. (2009), the only two pieces of study on private placement's long-run behavior and both drawing insights from *Under-reaction Hypothesis* and *Over-optimism Hypothesis*, yield different results. The former study documents negative long-term abnormal return but find it impossible to reconcile with positive announcement-period effect. *Under-reaction Hypothesis* does not apply since it implies positive long-run abnormal return. *Over-optimism Hypothesis* cannot hold either: The authors unfortunately find deteriorating operating performance of issuers immediately before private placements and are unable to justify over-optimism as Loughran and Ritter (1995) do.

On the other hand, Chou et al. (2009) claim that growth opportunity plays a vital role in validating *Over-optimism Hypothesis*. Empirically, they find only stocks of growth firms (indicated by high Tobin's Q) earn negative long-run abnormal returns. Theoretically, referring to Li and Lu (2010) and Barberis and Huang (2008), they argue that such negativity may arise from overinvestment by growth firms, positive skew-ness of small firms' stock return, or over-optimism on growth prospect. Evidence supports the last point.

2.5 Back to Tunneling: A Critique on the Literature

From the corporate governance point of view, tunneling should be seriously considered in any study on private placement. Firstly, there is ownership concentration. Not only are large shareholders influential over the decision of whether to place shares privately, they may also purchase shares and act as participants of influential negotiating power in an issue. Secondly, by default, participants of a private placement negotiate privately, without the monitoring of minor shareholders.[14] Thirdly but not finally, large shareholders may not share the same interests with small shareholders. All these concerns strike a sharp contrast against the lack of treatment of tunneling in extant studies.

Let's consider a possible scenario that the largest shareholder arbitrarily lowers offering price so as to purchase shares and gain more control rights at an unfairly low cost. Three factors contribute to researchers' indifference (or inability to identify tunneling) under this scenario. The first is information asymmetry problem. It can be plausibly declared that, since there is so much uncertainty about firm value that institutional investors are not willing to offer enough capital as the firm needs, the largest shareholder has to contribute capital and thus be given a low price for the sake of undertaking extraordinary risks. Existing studies are not able to falsify such a claim. The second is liquidity problem. Since privately placed shares are not allowed for resale for a certain period after the transaction, the largest shareholder can always claim that such a low price accurately reflects compensation to illiquidity of the holdings. It's impossible to price illiquidity in existing studies. The third is negative long-run performance. The controlling shareholder can claim it deserves the discount as the discount compensates its loss in the long run.

Baek et al. (2006) make the first and remarkable endeavor to reveal tunneling in private placements. As they put, 'the incentive for controlling shareholders to tunnel therefore tends to be strong in PSOs,[15] offering a natural context for powerful and convincing tunneling activity'. They study private placements in which both the purchaser and the issuer are listed firms belonging to the same business group, and find that upon announcement of an issue, the purchaser's stock price enjoys positive abnormal return while the issuer's price dips, evidence that wealth is tunneled from the issuing firm to the purchasing firm. Their study benefits from the unique business group structure in Korea and is able to circumvent the three problems aforementioned.

[14] There is a section at Wind's terminal dedicated to collect information on private placements that are proposed by the board of an issuer but not carried out in the end. This section, however, is empty, implying that in China the shareholders' meeting seldom rejects the board's proposal.

[15] PSO is the abbreviation for Private Securities Offering.

References

Anderson HD, Rose LC, Cahan SF (2006) Differential shareholder wealth and volume effects surrounding private equity placements in New Zealand. Pac-Basin Finan J 14:367–395

Baek J, Kang J, Lee I (2006) Business groups and tunneling: evidence from private securities offerings by Korean chaebols. J Finan 61:2415–2449

Bai C-E, Liu Q, Lu J, Song FM, Zhang J (2004) Corporate governance and market valuation in China. J Comp Econ 32:599–616

Barberis N, Huang M (2008) Stocks as lotteries: the implications of probability weighting for security prices. Am Econ Rev 98:2066–2100

Barclay MJ, Holderness CG, Sheehan DP (2007) Private placements and managerial entrenchment. J Corp Finan 13:461–484

Berle A, Means G (1932) The modern corporation and private property. Transaction Publishers, London

Booth JR, Smith RL (1986) Capital raising, underwriting and the certification hypothesis. J Finan Econ 15:261–281

Chen S-S, Hao KW, Lee C-F, Yeo GHH (2003) Wealth effects of private equity placements: evidence from Singapore. Finan Rev 37:165–183

Cheung Y-L, Raub PR, Stouraitis A (2006) Tunneling, propping, and expropriation: evidence from connected party transactions in Hong Kong. J Financ Econ 82:343–386

Chou D-W, Gombola M, Liu F-Y (2009) Long-run underperformance following private equity placements: the role of growth opportunities. Q Rev Econ Finan 49:1113–1128

Chung KH, Kim J-K (1999) Corporate ownership and the value of a vote in an emerging market. J Corp Finan 5:35–54

Claessens S, Djankov S, Fan J, Lang L (2002) Disentangling the incentive and entrenchment effects of large shareholders. J Finan 57:2741–2771

Cronqvist H, Nisson M (2005) The choice between rights offerings and private equity placements. J Finan Econ 78:375–407

Dann LY, DeAngelo H (1983) Standstill agreements, privately negotiated stock repurchases, and the market for corporate control. J Finan Econ 11:275–300

DeFusco RA, Johnson RR, Zorn TS (1990) The effect of executive stock option plans on stockholders and bondholders. J Finan 45:617–627

Dyck IJA, Zingales L (2002) Private benefits of control: an international comparison. CEPR Discussion Paper No. 3177, CEPR

Eckbo BE, Masulis RW (1992) Adverse selection and the rights offer paradox. J Finan Econ 32:293–332

Gao X (2008) The Marketing of Seasoned Equity Offerings, PhD Dissertation, The University of Florida

Handjinicolaou G, Kalay A (1984) Wealth redistributions or changes in firm value: an analysis of returns to bondholders and stockholders around dividend announcements. J Finan Econ 13:35–63

Hansen RS (1998) The demise of the rights issue. Rev Finan Stud 1:289–309

Hertzel M, Smith RL (1993) Market discounts and shareholder gains for placing equity privately. J Finan 48:459–485

Hertzel M, Lemmon M, Linck JS, Rees L (2002) Long-run performance following private placements of equity. J Finan 57:2595–2617

Janney JJ, Folta TB (2006) Moderating effects of investor experience on the signaling value of private equity placements. J Bus Ventur 21:27–44

Jensen MC, Meckling WH (1976) Theory of the firm: managerial behavior, agency costs and ownership structure. J Finan Econ 3:305–360

Jian M, Wong TJ (2003) Earnings management and tunneling through related party transactions: evidence from Chinese corporate groups. In: EFA 2003 annual conference, Paper No. 549, EFA

Johnson S, La Porta R, Lopez-de-Silanes F, Shleifer Andrei (2000) Tunneling. Am Econ Rev 90:22–27

Kahn C, Winton A (1998) Ownership structure, speculation, and shareholder intervention. J Finan 53:99–129
Kahneman D, Tversky A (1982) Judgment under uncertainty: heuristics and biases. Cambridge University Press, Cambridge
Kraus A, Stoll HR (1972) Price impacts of block trading on the New York stock exchange. J Finan 27:569–588
Krishnamurthy S, Spindt P, Subramaniam V, Woidtke T (2005) Does investor identity matter in equity issues? Evidence from private placements. J Finan Intermediation 14:210–238
La Porta R, Lopez-De-Silanes Florencio, Shleifer A (1999) Corporate ownership around the world. J Finan 54:471–517
Li D, Lu Z (2010) Does q-theory with investment frictions explain anomalies in the cross section of returns. J Finan Econ 98:297–314
Loughran T, Ritter JR (1995) The new issues puzzle. J Finan 50:23–51
Loughran T, Ritter J (1997) The operating performance of firms conducting seasoned equity offerings. J Finan 52:1823–1850
Marciukaityte D, Szewczyk SH, Varma R (2005) Investor overoptimism and private equity placements. J Finan Res 28:591–608
Michael BJ, Holderness CG (1989) Private benefits from control of public corporations. J Finan Econ 25:371–395
Mikkelson WH, Regassa H (2000) Premiums paid in block transactions. Manag Decis Econ 12:511–517
Morck R, Shleifer A, Vishny R (1988) Management ownership and market valuation: an empirical analysis. J Finan Econ 20:293–315
Myers S, Majluf NS (1984) Corporate financing and investment decisions when firms have information that investors do not have. J Finan Econ 13:187–221
Nicodano G, Sembenelli A (2004) Private benefits, block transaction premiums and ownership structure. Int Rev Finan Anal 13:227–244
Peng WQ, John Wei KC, Yang Z (2011) Tunneling or propping: evidence from connected transactions in China. J Corp Finan 17:306–325
Scholes MS (1972) The market for securities: substitution versus price pressure and the effects of information on share prices. J Bus 45:179–211
Shleifer A, Vishny RW (1986) Large shareholders and corporate control. J Polit Econ 94:461–488
Silber WL (1992) Discounts on restricted stock: the impact of illiquidity on stock prices. Finan Anal J 47:60–64
Smith CW (1977) Alternative methods for raising capital: rights versus underwritten offerings. J Finan Econ 5:273–307
Spiess DK, Affleck-Graves J (1995) Underperformance in long-run stock returns following seasoned equity offerings. J Financ Econ 38:243–267
Tan RSK, Chng PL, Tong YH (2002) Private placements and rights issues in Singapore. Pac Basin Finan J 10:29–54
Wruck KH (1989) Equity ownership concentration and firm value: evidence from private equity financings. J Finan Econ 23:3–28
Wruck KH, Wu Y (2002) Relationships, corporate governance, and performance: evidence from private placements of common stock. J Corp Finan 15:30–47
Wu Y (2004) The choice of equity-selling mechanisms. J Finan Econ 74:93–119
Wu X, Wang Z, Yao J (2005) Understanding the positive announcement effects of private equity placements: new insights from Hong Kong data. Rev Finan 9:385–414

Chapter 3
Choice of the Issuing Firm and Its Controlling Shareholder

Abstract In this chapter, I study which listed firms are more likely to choose private placement over SEO in refinancing. Firms whose controlling shareholder is state-owned and who want to establish business connections with potential investors are the most likely to conduct private placement. Then I look into the controlling shareholder's decision whether to purchase privately placed shares or not. The controlling shareholder does not care about holdings dilution caused by not participating in a private placement. No matter how severe information asymmetry is on the issuer's true value, there are always institutional investors contributing capital to it, so the largest shareholder does not have to participate in the offering for the sake of solving under-investment problem.

Keywords Private placement • PIPE • Choice • Logit • Information asymmetry

Studies on choice of equity refinancing methods mostly focus on the choice between rights offering and SEO, both public ones. The choice between the alternatives of seasoned public offering and private placement, however, has gained inadequate attention. In striking contrast is the increasingly prominent domination of private placement over SEO and rights issue in China's capital market since May 2006, when CSRC issued *Regulatory Measures of Securities Issuance for Listed Firms* and formally introduced private placement as a feasible equity refinancing method in China.

Up to December 31 2011, a total of 715 listed firms have raised additional capital through private placements, accounting for 82 % of all firms conducting seasoned financing. Since May of 2006, private placements have gathered a total of 1,142 billion Chinese Yuan, accounting for 78 % of capital raised through equity refinancing. Obviously, in terms of number of firms involved and the scale of capital raised, private placement has become the foremost important means of equity refinancing; and it takes a short time for the dominance to take place.[1] It naturally follows that my first step in analyzing private placement in China is to

[1] There were 137 private placements, but only 23 rights issue and 30 seasoned public offerings in 2007.

P. Song, *Private Placement of Public Equity in China*, SpringerBriefs in Finance,
DOI: 10.1007/978-3-642-55093-5_3, © The Author(s) 2014

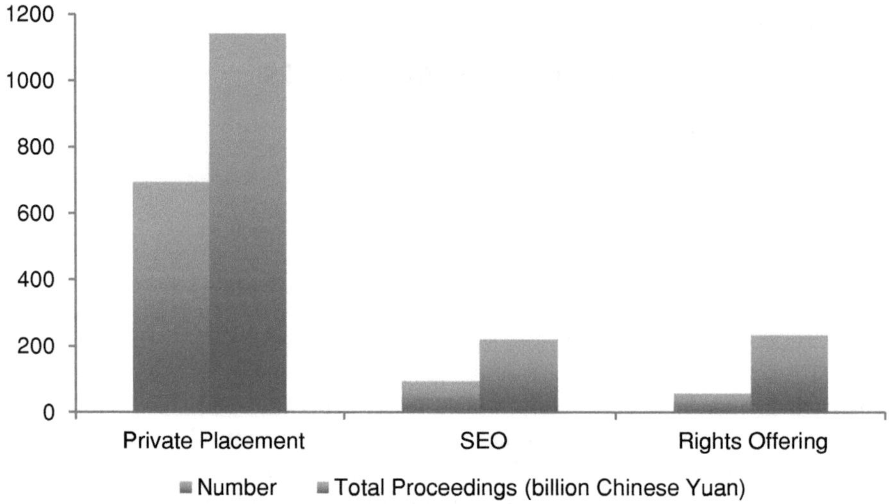

Fig. 3.1 Weights of the three equity refinancing methods in China. This figure shows total number and total proceeds of private placements, SEOs and right offerings between 2007 and 2011. The column on the *left* shows total number. The column on the *right* shows total proceeds that are measured in billion Chinese Yuan. Since underwriting fees are minimal compared to total proceeds, I find it unnecessary to display total net proceeds here. All data are extracted from Wind terminal using the date screener called "Primary Market"

compare it with seasoned public offering and determine which firms are more likely to conduct private placements.

It should be noted that in this chapter I only make a comparison between private placement and SEO by listed firms in China. I do not consider rights offering albeit it still plays a role in equity refinancing. Rights offering's domain has been gradually encroached by SEO since 1999 when CSRC approved the latter as an equity refinancing method.[2] It was the first equity refinancing method used in China and indeed popular in the 1990s, but the popularity has been decreasing, especially after the split-share reform. As Fig. 3.1 shows, from 2007 to 2011, the number of rights offerings in China's stock market accounts for just 6.6 % of all equity refinancing campaigns. What's more, capital collected through rights offering is merely 10.60 % of all raised through equity refinancing. I believe that a comparison between the top two methods can offer enough insights as to the choice of a listed firm in need of additional equity.

3.1 Hypothesis Development

In this section, I develop hypotheses concerning firstly the firm's choice between private placement and SEO and secondly the firm's largest shareholder's decision of whether to purchase shares given that the firm has decided to conduct a

[2] CSRC introduced seasoned public offering to the capital market in 1999.

private placement. I draw insights from the ownership structure hypothesis and the information asymmetry hypothesis discussed in Chap. 2, and consider unique features of listed firms in China.

3.1.1 A Firm's Choice Between Private Placement and SEO

In both private placements and SEOs, the controlling shareholder of the issuer enjoys priority in shares allocation in case of over-subscription. That's to say, the controlling shareholder should be indifferent between a private placement and an SEO: In either case, it can participate if afraid of ownership being diluted after the offering or stand away if glad to lose some ownership. Thus, ownership structure does not matter in a firm's decision to conduct private placement or SEO, but I conjecture that ownership property does matter.

The development of China's capital market till now can be divided into two phases: Before and after the stock-split reform. Initially, since the capital market was of small scale and state-owned enterprises were pressed by historic burdens,[3] only the best quality part of a stated-owned enterprise's assets could be listed. As the stock-split reform approached to an end, CSRC and State-owned Asset Committee of the State Council initiated a campaign to push more quality state-owned assets to the public market by issuing *Advice on Improving the Quality of Listed Firms, Advice on Restructuring State-owned Assets and State-owned Listed Firms*, and so on. The authority encourages qualified state-owned enterprises to be listed as a whole. If a state-owned firm does not qualify to be on the public market as a whole, it is advised to inject its quality assets into suitable listed firms. In this age of full circulation, large shareholders of listed firms no longer focus on enlarging net assets, the maximization of which usually appears when financial theorists model a listed firm's behavior in China before the split-share reform, but are motivated to pursue profit and promote market value of their firms. Listed state-owned enterprises are no exception; these firms are more encouraged than ever to pursue profitability by securitizing unlisted quality assets.

Both small shareholders and institutional investors welcome private placements by state-owned firms. It is required that new shares privately placed be restricted from trading by one to three years. In this case, purchasers of privately placed shares, such as incumbent large shareholders and institutional investors, need to focus on intrinsic value of the issuer and long-run prospects. Such focus on the long run is aligned with listed state-owned enterprises' goal of preserving and promoting the value of state assets. Naturally the small shareholder would regard a private placement justifiable and acceptable.

Not only are state-owned firms in favor of private placements, CSRC as the stock market regulator is also more willing to approve private placement applications from

---

[3] Burdens include maintaining high welfare benefits to employees, being restrained from firing inefficient workers, and undertaking not-for-profit projects, et al.

state-owned firms than these from private firms. Politically it is in CRSC's interest to cater to the State Council's guidance on promoting more state-owned assets onto the exchange. In fact, it takes on average 17 days for an application from state-owned firms to be approved by CRSC, but 29 days for a private firm to get permission. The 12-day difference is not negligible considering efficient use of capital.

Analysis above leads to the *Ownership Property Hypothesis*:

H1: If the controlling shareholder of a firm is state-owned rather than private, then the firm is more likely to conduct private placement than SEO.

According to Myers and Majluf (1984), due to information asymmetry between firm insiders and public investors on firm value, SEO is considered a signal of firm value overestimation by the market. Firm management would give up investment opportunities of positive NPV rather than raising additional funds through equity offering, a phenomenon called underinvestment. However, if firm management is able to signal to the market true value of the firm with a low cost, or if outside investors are capable of evaluating intrinsic value of the firm, then the underinvestment problem can be effectively solved. Eckbo and Masulis (1992) show that by employing an underwriter, a firm conducting rights offering sends to the market a signal that firm value is justified. Thus underwritten rights offerings are good means of reducing information asymmetry and the cost of adverse selection.

However, the underwriter's signal in a rights offering is only credible when information asymmetry is moderate. As information asymmetry on firm value becomes more severe, neither rights offering nor SEO is able to solve the underinvestment problem. As Hertzel and Smith (1993) first point out, private placement becomes a feasible choice for firms wanting additional financing but facing greater information asymmetry problem.

The analysis above applies to China's equity raising practice too. If information asymmetry on firm value is relatively moderate, it is easier to make small investors participate in a public offering of the firm. In this case, the firm does not have to sell shares privately. If, on the other hand, information asymmetry regarding firm value is severe, compared to small investors, it is institutional investors that are more capable of determining the true value of the firm (Grinblatt and Titman 2002; Gibson et al. 2004). In this case, firm management can only solve the underinvestment problem by placing shares to interested institutional investors, namely by initiating a private placement of equity. The *Information Asymmetry Hypothesis* regarding a listed firm's choice follows naturally:

H2: The more severe the information asymmetry problem of a firm, the more likely the firm uses private placement to refinance equity.

My next hypothesis draws insights from Cronqvist and Nisson (2005). They are the first to introduce the notion of business connection to the literature on seasoned public offering. They propose that, besides raising additional capital, firms may also establish business connections through seasoned offerings. This is easily understandable: A firm can effectively align the interest of its supplier with its own by selling shares to the supplier.

In practice, it is easier to establish a business relation through private placement than through public offering. In a private placement, shares can be sold directly to the investor with whom the issuer is willing to build a business connection; the investor does not have to worry about not getting its targeted amount of shares. In a public offering, the investor can be guaranteed with desired shares only when it is an incumbent shareholder. I assume that the investor is not an incumbent shareholder for an obvious reason: The firm does not have to connect with an investor if the investor already serves as its shareholder. The third hypothesis, *Business Connection Hypothesis*, is stated below.

H3: Firms intending to establish a business connection with other business entities at the time of issuance are more likely to choose private placement than SEO.

3.1.2 The Largest Shareholder's Decision to Participate in a Private Placement

Now I assume that a firm has decided to conduct a private placement and proceed to consider its controlling shareholder's choice of whether to purchase shares or not.

Claessens et al. (2000) find that in Eastern Asia, there are a large number of firms controlled by families through the pyramidal ownership structure,[4] which endows the controlling family with more voting rights than cash flow rights. Such discrepancy leads to what Dyck and Zingales (2002) call benefits from control rights. Therefore, the controlling shareholder's incentive to prevent its holding from being diluted and to maintain control rights plays an important role in the equity refinancing practice. In an SEO, current shareholders are given the priority to purchase shares in case of oversubscription. In a private placement, the controlling shareholder can decide to purchase shares or not. As a result, from the perspective of preventing holding dilution, the controlling shareholder does not care which equity refinancing method to use: It has enough degree of freedom to purchase wanted shares under both methods.

Although the controlling shareholder is indifferent between SEO and private placement, considering its willingness to prevent its holdings from being diluted, I conjecture that its choice of whether to participate in a private placement does vary according to its percentage of shareholding. The *Anti-dilution Hypothesis* follows:

H4: The likelihood for a controlling shareholder to participate in a private placement is decreasing in the controlling shareholder's percentage of holding prior to the placement.

Finally, I propose that information asymmetry regarding firm value also plays a role when the largest shareholder considers whether to purchase shares in the

[4] Under pyramidal ownership structure, an entrepreneur sets up a new firm to be under the control of a firm that he/she already owns. This is in contrast to the horizontal ownership structure, where an entrepreneur sets up new firms that he/she directly controls.

private placement. In the previous section, I have discussed the pecking order of equity refinancing methods in solving the underinvestment problem: As information becomes more asymmetric, underwriters in rights offerings or SEOs no longer send any credible signal to the market and institutional investors in private placements begin to play the role of certifying firm value.

It's possible that the issuing firm's true value is so difficult to determine that even sophisticated institutional investors would not like to participate in the private placement. In this case, it is no longer feasible to solve the underinvestment problem by introducing outside investors to the firm, and if firm management and interested large shareholders really would not like to forgo profitable investment opportunities, they have to inject capital to the firm by themselves. That is to say, as information asymmetry goes to extremity such that only insiders like incumbent large shareholders are able to determine firm value, a private placement to these shareholders becomes the only feasible way of overcoming the underinvestment problem. Thus I have the following *Information Asymmetry Hypothesis*:

H5: The more severe the information asymmetry problem of the issuing firm is, the more likely that the controlling shareholder participates in the private placement.

3.2 Data

3.2.1 Sample Selection

On May 8th, 2006, CRSC formally approved private placement of public equity as an applicable method of equity refinancing. To make better comparisons between SEO and private placement in China and considering data availability,[5] I target firms that conducted private placements between 2007 and 2011 and only consider firms that are listed in Shanghai and Shenzhen's A-share markets.[6] I arrive at the final sample by the following procedure.

Firstly, using data screener called *Primary Market* on Wind's financial data terminal, I obtain a total of 715 observations of private placements. I would like to eliminate firms that have also conducted SEOs or rights offerings during the observation period. This leads to deletion of 28 observations. Next I delete observations in the financial services industry since they behave differently from firms in other industries. Fifteen observations are eliminated in this step. Lastly I drop 2 observations whose shareholder information is missing.

5 Detailed information on transactions completed in 2006 is not available in electronic formats.

6 Transactions that take place in China's B-share stock market are not considered in this study. There are only a small number of equity refinancing activities on the market. I do not pool these activities with transactions on the A-share market.

Table 3.1 Process of sample construction

Panel A	
	Private placements
Original observations	715
Delete: Multi-refinancing observations	28
Delete: Financial firms	15
Delete: No share-holding data	2
Final sample	670
Controlling shareholder participation	321
Purchase by assets	193
Purchase by cash	128
Panel B	
	SEOs
Original observations	94
Delete: Multi-refinancing observations	21
Final sample	83

This table shows the data filtering process to reach the final sample I use in Chap. 3. All data are extracted from Wind terminal via data screener "Primary Market". Multi-refinancing observations are these also observed to conduct SEOs or rights offerings between 2007 and 2011. I also delete observations absent of share-holding data and observations in the financial services industry, for this industry behaves differently from others. For private placement observations, I also count the number of them in which the controlling shareholder participates, purchases by assets and purchases by cash

Secondly, I obtain a total of 94 observations of SEOs. I drop 6 observations that also conducted rights offerings and 15 observations that also privately placed shares during observation period 2007–2011.

Table 3.1 shows the whole process of sample construction.

As shown in Table 3.1, there are 670 private placement observations in my sample. 642 listed firms conducted these private placements. In the observation period, there are 6 firms that each did three private placements and 14 firms that each completed two private placements. Two points are worth mentioning. Firstly, there are 321 private placements in which the largest shareholder of the issuing firm purchased shares. Secondly, assets are used to buy shares in 193 observations while cash is used in the remaining 128 cases. There are 83 public offerings in the sample. Since there are two firms that each implemented two public offerings, 81 firms are observed in the sample.

3.2.2 Sample Statistics

I extract details of all transactions and firm fundamentals from the Wind terminal. How I collect data specifically can be found in notes to tables. In Table 3.2, I show statistics of the sample across industries and years.

Table 3.2 Subsamples of private placements and SEOs

Industry	Private placement				SEO			
	N	Percent	MV	Proceed	N	Percent	MV	Proceed
Panel A: Private placements and SEOs across industries								
Agriculture, forestry, husbandry and fishery	13	1.94	5.82	7.21	0	0	–	–
Architecture	17	2.54	7.47	1.19	3	3.61	3.10	0.64
Information technology	34	5.10	9.17	0.77	2	2.41	4.06	0.76
Media and culture	6	0.90	1.80	0.79	0	0	–	–
Mining	20	2.99	24.92	0.90	1	1.20	15.27	0.63
Manufacturing (9 sub-sectors)	380	56.72	10.17	1.43	59	71.10	12.26	1.54
Electronics	41	6.12	5.21	1.75	6	7.23	3.30	1.21
Food and beverage	23	3.43	7.94	0.40	3	3.61	6.06	0.70
Limber and furniture	14	2.01	4.07	0.55	0	0	–	–
Machinery, equipment and apparatus	146	21.80	25.70	2.97	31	37.35	22.02	3.64
Metal	31	4.63	24.92	0.70	2	2.41	17.79	3.15
Paper and printing	18	2.69	7.49	1.39	0	0	–	–
Petro and chemistry	26	3.88	12.95	0.86	5	6.02	15.61	1.15
Pharm and biological engineering	37	5.52	7.24	1.30	5	6.02	6.77	1.22
Textile, apparel and leather	44	6.57	9.90	1.90	7	8.43	9.69	1.15
Other	17	2.54	7.49	1.39	0	0	–	–
Realty	66	9.85	9.08	2.30	9	10.84	24.38	4.28
Social Service	16	2.39	6.95	1.49	1	1.20	9.58	0.45
Transportation and logistics	29	4.33	20.88	3.44	3	3.61	43.61	6.48
Utilities	34	5.07	17.15	2.97	4	4.82	29.66	4.26
Wholesale and retailing	38	5.67	8.69	1.23	1	1.20	5.76	0.71
Total	670	100	10.67	1.65	83	100	14.53	1.99

Year	Private placement				SEO			
	N	Percent	MV	Proceed	N	Percent	MV	Proceed
Panel B: Private placements and SEOs across years								
2007	132	19.70	15.10	1.97	26	31.33	15.26	1.46
2008	99	14.78	9.00	0.91	25	30.12	13.27	1.85
2009	112	16.72	9.46	1.06	12	14.46	9.01	1.25
2010	147	21.94	7.84	1.08	11	13.25	22.54	3.77
2011	180	26.86	11.43	2.68	9	10.84	15.13	2.90
Total	670	100	10.67	1.65	83	100	14.53	1.99

(continued)

Table 3.2 (continued)

	N	Percent	MV	Proceed
Panel C: Private placements and SEOs across shareholder types and means of purchase				
Private placement				
Largest shareholder participation	321	47.91	12.53	2.13
Purchase by cash	158	23.58	11.29	1.51
Purchase by assets	163	24.33	13.74	2.72
No Largest shareholder participation	349	52.09	9.06	1.23
SEO				
Largest shareholder participation	28	33.73	16.46	2.55
No largest shareholder participation	55	66.27	13.68	1.74

This table describes private placements and SEOs across industries and years. N means the number of private placements or SEOs. Percent is calculated as N/Total number of corresponding offerings. For any observation, its market value is the average value of 30 trading days prior to the board announcement date. I retrieve a firm's market value from Wind using entry S_VAL_MV. MV is then calculated as the average of all observations' market value. Proceed is the average raw proceeds of all offerings. Raw proceeds are extracted from Wind terminal using data screener "Primary Market". Both MV and Proceed are measured in billion Chinese Yuan. Since underwriting fees of private placements and SEOs are minimal compared to raw proceeds, I find it unnecessary to present net proceeds here

Panel A of Table 3.2 displays statistics of transactions across industries. Listed firms that conduct SEOs cluster in Manufacturing, a gross industry consisting of nine sub-sectors. More than 71 % of SEO observations fall into the manufacturing industry. While firms choosing private placement scatter more across industries, more than 56 % of them are also in Manufacturing. Panel B of Table 3.2 displays statistics of transactions across years. It's obvious that each year, there are significantly more private placements than SEOs in absolute number. The difference enlarged from 106 in 2007 to 171 in 2001. In terms of number of transactions, private placement activities experienced a decrease of 25 % in 2008, but gained traction again in 2010 and 2011. The number of SEOs, however, has been decreasing for consecutively five years, ending up at merely nine in 2011.

Panel A also shows that private placement firms have a higher average market value than their SEO counterparts in nine industries but are smaller in six industries. Private placement firms have more average proceeds per transaction in eight industries, but smaller ones in seven industries. Panel B shows on a yearly basis, however, private placement firms are generally smaller and gather less proceeds than SEO firms.

Tan et al. (2002) report the average market value of private placement firms in Singapore as 0.47 billion Singapore Dollars (approximately 2.36 billion Chinese Yuan).[7] The number for Hong Kong as documented in Wu et al. (2005) is 1.57 billion

[7] Due to impossibility to match observation period of our samples, I transform currencies to USD using rough estimates of exchange rate. No matter how rough my estimation is, it does not change the general picture. I do not compare my sample with these in Wruck (1989) and other older studies, since it's meaningless to make a comparison between so apart observation periods.

Hong Kong Dollars (approximately the same amount as Chinese Yuan). My data show that private placement firms in China are much bigger than their Singapore or Hong Kong counterparts. It's also true that these firms in China grab much more proceeds than the other two regions. For limited space, I do not elaborate here.

Panel C of Table 3.2 reveals that the controlling shareholder purchases shares in roughly half of private placements. To the contrary, the largest shareholder participates in about 1/3 of SEOs. In a private placement, the largest shareholder purchases shares by cash or assets with about the same occurrence.

3.3 Methodologies and Variable Construction

In this section, I utilize Logit models to test the five hypotheses developed in Sect. 3.2.

I denote the dependent variable used to test hypotheses 1–3 as a dummy variable *pp* (private placement). If a private placement is conducted in observation i, then $pp_i = 1$. If, instead, a public offering is observed in i, then $pp_i = 0$. Whether the largest shareholder of a firm conducting private placement purchases shares in the offering, namely the dependent variable used to test hypotheses 4 and 5, is denoted as *lsp* (largest shareholder participation). If the largest shareholder in observation i participates in the private offering, then $lsp_i = 1$. Otherwise, $lsp_i = 0$.

To test Hypothesis 1, I construct an independent variable *property* (ownership property), which is set to 1 if the largest shareholder of the firm is state-owned and 0 if the largest shareholder is private. As discussed, I conjecture that a state-owned listed firm is more likely to conduct a private placement than an SEO due to the issuer's own preference and CSRC's preferential treatment.

To test Hypothesis 2, I make use of five independent variables, *frac*, *size*, *bm*, *hitech*, and *age* to proxy information asymmetry regarding firm value.

Variable *frac* denotes relative size of the placement and is calculated as shares issued in the private placement or SEO divided by shares outstanding after the transaction. Hertzel and Smith (1993) equate *frac* with the amount of efforts needed in determining whether proceeds from the offering would be profitably used and assume that a higher *frac* means a higher level of information asymmetry. I follow their reasoning and expect that if *frac* is higher, then the firm is more likely to perform a private placement in equity refinancing.

Variable *size* denotes size of the issuing firm and is calculated as log of the firm's total assets at the end of the year immediately preceding the transaction. As widely assumed, it is more difficult to determine the prospect and true value of a small firm than a big one. Moreover, there are generally less stock analysts covering small firms than large ones. Thus, I conjecture that the likelihood of a firm conducting private placement is decreasing in *size*.

Variable *bm* is the book-to-market ratio of the firm. After Hertzel and Smith (1993) introduce *bm* to proxy information asymmetry into the private placement literature, such a variable has been widely used. A high book-to-market ratio means the firm's intangible value is relatively small compared to the tangible value. Since generally it is harder to determine intangible value than tangible value, a high book-to-market ratio is regarded as indicator of a low level of information asymmetry. As a result, I conjecture that the inclination of a firm to choose private placement is decreasing in *bm*.

frac, *size*, and *bm* are three popular proxies for information asymmetry in private placement literature. To follow Cronqvist and Nisson (2005), I add another variable *hitech*, a dummy; it is set to 1 if the firm is in the industries of Electronics, Information Technology, and Pharmaceuticals and Biological Engineering, and 0 if not. I assume it is more costly to determine the true value of a high-technology firm and that it is more likely for such a firm to choose private placement over SEO.

My last independent variable to proxy information asymmetry is *age*, which is widely used in China and is the number of years that a firm has been listed. It's easily understandable that the longer a firm has been on the exchange, the more familiar investors are with it and the less uncertainty on firm value. Therefore, I expect the probability that a firm conducts private placement to be decreasing in *age*.

To test Hypothesis 3, I construct a dummy variable *connection* to denote if any investor in an offering is a potential business partner with the issuer. Referring to *Detailed Statement* of each offering, I set *connection* to 1 if the section titled *Potential Relationship of the Investor to the Issuer* is not empty, and 0 otherwise. As discussed, it is easier for an investor to get targeted amount of shares through a private placement than an SEO; so hypothetically, *connection* should have a positive sign in my Logit models.

As independent variables, *abscon* and *lsper* are used to test Hypothesis 4. *abscon* is a dummy variable that equals 1 if the largest shareholder has absolute control over the firm, or owns 50 % or more shares outstanding prior to the offering. If the largest shareholder owns less than 50 % of the firm, then $abscon = 0$. I argue that if the largest shareholder owns a large percentage of a firm, it would not consider ownership dilution a serious problem and may not participate in the private placement. Put in another way, a shareholder fully controlling the firm may give up a little control right in exchange for funding by institutional investors. The expected sign of *abscon* is negative. *lsper*, which is the largest shareholder's percentage of ownership, is simply measured by the percentage of shares outstanding the largest shareholder owns prior to the transaction. I assume that the larger *lsper* is, the less that the largest shareholder averts share dilution and expect the probability that the largest shareholder purchases shares in a private placement to be decreasing in *lsper*.

To test Hypothesis 5, I make use of the five information asymmetry variables already discussed: *frac*, *size*, *bm*, *hitech* and *age*. Hypothesis 5 purports that the more uncertainty on firm value, the more likely that the largest shareholder participates in the private placement. Therefore, I expect the likelihood of the largest shareholder's participation to be increasing in *frac* and *hitech*, but decreasing in *size*, *bm* and *age*.

Table 3.3 exhibits expected signs of variables.

Table 3.3 Variables and expected signs

Variable	Hypothesis related	Expected sign
Panel A: The firm's choice		
pp	–	
property	Ownership property	+
frac	Information asymmetry	+
size	Information asymmetry	–
bm	Information asymmetry	–
hitech	Information asymmetry	+
age	Information asymmetry	–
connection	Business connection	+
Panel B: The largest shareholder's choice		
lsp	–	
lsper	Anti-dilution	–
abscon	Anti-dilution	–
frac	Information asymmetry	+
size	Information asymmetry	–
bm	Information asymmetry	–
hitech	Information asymmetry	+
age	Information asymmetry	–

This table shows variables used to test hypotheses and their expected signs in Chap. 3. *pp* is a dummy variable set to 1 if a transaction is observed to be a private placement. *lsp* is a dummy variable set to 1 if the largest shareholder of an issuer participates in the offering. *property* is a dummy variable set to 1 if the controlling shareholder of the issuer is state-owned. *frac* is calculated as shares issued over shares outstanding after the issue. *size* is the log of total assets of the issuer prior to the offering, measured in billion Chinese Yuan. *bm* is the book-to-market ratio widely used in literature. *hitech* is a dummy variable set to 1 if the issuer is in industries of Electronics, IT and Pharmaceutical and Biological Engineering. *age* is calculated by subtracting year of the offering by year the issuer went public. *connection* is a dummy variable set to 1 if the issuer has potential business relations with investors. Data on *property* and *connection* are collected by hand from reading *Detailed Statement* of each offering. All other data are extracted from Wind

3.4 Empirical Tests

3.4.1 Descriptive Statistics and Mean-Difference Analysis

I present descriptive statistics of my sample in Table 3.4. The whole sample is divided into two subsamples, one containing private placement observations and the other SEO observations, presented in Panel A and Panel B respectively.

Panel A shows that in 43 % of private placement observations, the largest shareholder is a state-owned entity. On average, new shares issued in a private placement account for 17 % of shares outstanding after the offering. The average size of a private placement firm measured by total assets is 3.98 billion Yuan ($10^{9.6}$ equals 3.98 billion). A typical private placement firm has a book-to-market ratio of 0.23 and has been listed in the market for an average of 8.18 years when conducting the refinancing. High-technology firms account for 19 % of private placement observations. Business connections between the issuer and investors are established in 29 % of all private

Table 3.4 Descriptive statistics and mean analysis

Variable	N	Mean	Median	Std Error	Minimum	Maximum
Panel A: Private placements						
property	670	0.43	0	0.49	0	1
frac	670	17 %	11 %	15 %	1 %	79 %
size	670	9.60	9.46	0.56	8.37	11.36
bm	670	0.23	0.18	0.27	−0.03	3.54
hitech	670	0.19	0	0.39	0	1
age	670	8.18	8	3.9	1	16
connection	670	0.29	0	0.45	0	1
abscon	670	0.49	0	0.50	0	1
lsper	670	0.39	0.40	0.17	0.07	0.79
Panel B: SEOs						
property	83	0.19	0	0.40	0	1
frac	83	0.08	0.07	0.06	0.01	0.29
size	83	9.79	9.72	0.48	9.09	10.97
bm	83	0.49	0.43	0.24	0.13	1.10
hitech	83	0.15	0	0.37	0	1
age	83	5.9	5	3.50	1	15
connection	83	0.11	0	0.31	0	1

	Private placements		SEOs		Difference (*p* -value)
	N	Mean	N	Mean	
Panel C: Difference analysis on firm's choice					
property	670	0.43	83	0.19	0.24 (0.00)
frac	670	0.17	83	0.08	0.09 (0.00)
size	670	9.60	83	9.79	−0.19 (0.73)
bm	670	0.23	83	0.49	−0.26 (0.19)
hitech	670	0.19	83	0.15	0.04 (0.52)
age	670	8.18	83	5.90	2.28 (0.0)

(continued)

Table 3.4 (continued)

	Private placements		SEOs		Difference (p -value)
	N	Mean	N	Mean	
connection	670	0.29	83	0.11	0.19 (0.00)

	$lsp = 0$		$lsp = 1$		Difference (p -value)
	N	Mean	N	Mean	
Panel D: Difference analysis (largest shareholder's choice)					
abscon	321	0.48	349	0.51	0.03 (0.62)
lsper	321	39.35	349	37.89	−1.46 (0.55)
frac	321	0.17	349	0.22	0.05 (0.23)
size	321	9.44	349	9.78	0.34 (0.71)
bm	321	0.24	349	0.23	−0.01 (0.89)
hitech	321	0.24	349	0.17	−0.07 (0.08)
age	321	7.56	349	8.88	1.32 (0.00)

This table shows descriptive statistics for subsamples of private placements and SEOs. Mean-difference analysis is conducted in panels C and D. The value of *property* is determined manually by reading *Detailed Statement* of each transaction. *frac* is calculated by shares offered in the offering and shares outstanding immediately after the offering. The former number is obtained from Wind's data screener "Primary Market", while the later using entry S_SHARE_TOTAL. I use S_FA_TA to obtain the value of *size*. I use S_Val_BPS to retrieve book value and S_Val_MV to retrieve market value, so as to calculate *bm* by division. The value of *hitech* is determined manually by checking if an issuer belongs to the industries of Electronics, IT and Pharmaceutical and Biological Engineering. I use S_INFO_LDATE to retrieve the year when an issuer went public. The year of offering is available from data screener "Primary Market". Subtraction results in *age*. The value of *connection* is determined manually by reading *Detailed Statement* of each transaction. Finally I use S_HOLDER_PCT to retrieve the value of *lsper*

offerings. Finally, immediately before these offerings, a typical largest shareholder holds 39 % of shares outstanding of the issuer, strongly indicating the existence of a controlling shareholder in China's listed firms. Panel B displays the same set of information for SEO observations in my sample.

In Panel C, I calculate the difference between the mean of each interested variable for both subsamples. As *p*-values tell, *propert*, *frac*, *age* and *connection* are very likely to have explanatory power on the firm's choice between private placement and SEO. Difference analysis in Panel D shows that *hitech* and *age* can possibly explain more of the largest shareholder's choice of participating or not than other independent variables.

3.4.2 Regression Analysis

Table 3.5 shows results of Logit regressions of the firm' choice on independent variables and control variables.[8]

In all regressions, *property* is significantly positive at 1 % level. This is strong evidence that a listed firm with a state-owned controlling shareholder is more likely to choose private placement over SEO when in need of refinancing. It seems listed firms whose controlling shareholders are state-owned are reacting rationally to CSRC's preferential treatment in approving private offering applications. This finding, although may not be applicable to other stock markets rather than China, is new to the literature on the choice among equity refinancing methods.

Hypothesis 3, which says a listed firm wanting to be connected to an investor in business is more likely to undertake private offering, is also supported by regression results. Independent variable *connection* is significantly positive at 1 % level in five regressions and at 5 % level in one regression. This result offers a supportive hand to what Cronqvist and Nisson (2005) have documented in their study on the choice between private placement and rights offering in Sweden.

Proxies for information asymmetry offer contrary evidence regarding Hypothesis 2. On the one hand, variables *frac* and *size* are significantly different from zero and have expected signs. On the other hand, the coefficient of *age* is unexpectedly significantly larger than zero, telling that the longer an issuer has been public, the more likely it chooses private offering over SEO. The sign of *age* contradicts the *Information Asymmetry Hypothesis*. In contrast to Cronqvist and Nisson (2005) who find that *Information Asymmetry Hypothesis* works in Sweden's capital market, I am not able to support the notion that in China the more the public knows the issuer, the less likely the issuer chooses private placement.

In summary, I find strong evidence for the *Ownership Property Hypothesis* and the *Business Connection Hypothesis*, the first unique to China and the second offering supports to the Swedish case. The *Information Asymmetry Hypothesis*, however, is challenged by one of the proxies.

---

[8] To follow the main stream and facilitate comparison, I use ROE (return on equity) and leverage (debt/(debt + equity)) as control variables. I've also tried other control variables whenever possible, but found no much difference in regression results.

Table 3.5 Regression results on firm choice

	1	2	3	4	5	6
Intercept	1.8384*** (4.20)	1.7874*** (3.66)	0.6675*** (10.84)	1.4997*** (3.06)	0.6686*** (10.76)	1.7958*** (3.67)
property	0.1489*** (2.87)	0.1472*** (2.81)	0.1793*** (3.15)			0.1489*** (2.83)
frac	0.5818*** (3.28)	0.5771*** (3.17)		0.6251*** (3.35)		0.5781*** (3.17)
size	−0.1324*** (−2.81)	−0.1264** (−2.30)		−0.0914* (−1.66)		−0.1280** (−2.32)
bm	−0.4487*** (−5.35)	−0.4478*** (−5.08)		−0.4964*** (−5.53)		−0.4447*** (−5.01)
hitech				0.0268 (0.42)		0.0255 (0.41)
age	0.0202*** (3.14)	0.0212*** (3.25)		0.0245*** (3.71)		0.0209*** (3.20)
connection	0.1507*** (2.80)	0.1460*** (2.65)			0.1678*** (2.65)	0.1439*** (2.60)
roe		0.0488 (0.23)	0.2274 (1.02)	0.0940 (0.43)	0.1452 (0.63)	0.0505 (0.24)
leverage		−0.04777 (−0.36)	0.0048 (0.04)	−0.0985 (−0.06)	0.1046 (0.79)	−0.0398 (−0.30)
Year control	Yes	Yes	Yes	Yes	Yes	Yes
LR Chi^2	17.09	12.58	4.00	11.76	3.03	11.16
Pseudo R^2	0.2860	0.2802	0.0362	0.2404	0.0248	0.2776
Observations	753	753	753	753	753	753

This table shows Logit regression results of firm choice on various independent variables. The value of *property* is determined manually by reading *Detailed Statement* of each transaction. *frac* is calculated by shares offered in the offering and shares outstanding immediately after the offering. The former number is obtained from Wind's data screener "Primary Market", while the later using entry S_SHARE_TOAL. I use S_FA_TA to obtain the value of *size*. I use S_FA_BPS to retrieve book value and S_VAL_MV to retrieve market value, so as to calculate *bm* by division. The value of *hitech* is determined manually by checking if an issuer belongs to the industries of Electronics, IT and Pharmaceutical and Biological Engineering. I use S_INFO_LDATE to retrieve the year when an issuer went public. The year of offering is available from data screener "Primary Market". Subtraction results in *age*. The value of *connection* is determined manually by reading *Detailed Statement* of each transaction. Finally I use S_HOLDER_PCT to retrieve the value of *lsper*. I use *roe* and *leverage* as control variables. *roe* is return on common equity the year before the issue, retrieved by S_FA_ROE, while *leverage* is calculated as debt over the sum of debt and equity. Debt-to-equity ratio is obtained by S_FA_RATIODE

Z-statistics are listed in the parentheses to the right of coefficients

Significance levels of 1, 5 and 10 % are denoted by ***, ** and * respectively

Table 3.6 Regression results on largest shareholder choice

	1	2	3	4	5	6
Intercept	-2.0135^{***} (−3.38)	-1.6683^{***} (−2.52)		0.3667^{***} (2.78)	-2.0193^{***} (−2.99)	-2.0803^{***} (−3.10)
lsper				−0.0052 (−1.30)		−0.0009 (−0.45)
abscon				0.1632 (1.21)	0.0319 (0.45)	
frac			0.9007 (0.68)		0.9207 (0.69)	0.8802 (0.53)
size	0.2613^{***} (4.22)	0.2162^{***} (2.98)	0.2459^{***} (3.28)		0.2397^{***} (3.14)	0.2527^{***} (3.30)
bm			−0.0418 (−0.32)		−0.0455 (−0.35)	−0.0394 (−0.30)
hitech	-0.1665^{**} (−1.87)	−0.1495 (−1.64)	-0.1510^{*} (−1.70)		-0.1531^{*} (−1.72)	-0.1513^{*} (−1.70)
age			0.0045 (0.49)		0.0049 (0.52)	0.0042 (0.45)
roe		−0.0408 (−0.14)	−0.0452 (−0.15)	0.2829 (0.94)	−0.0528 (−0.30)	−0.0256 (−0.09)
leverage		0.2548 (1.36)	0.0584 (0.30)	0.3667^{***} (2.94)	0.0581 (0.30)	0.0508 (0.26)
Year Control	Yes	Yes	Yes	Yes	Yes	Yes
LR Chi^2	11.09	5.80	5.90	3.26	5.16	5.16
Pseudo R^2	0.0978	0.0945	0.1585	0.0468	0.1546	0.1546
Observations	670	670	670	670	670	670

This table shows Logit regression results of the largest shareholder's choice on various independent variables. The value of *property* is determined manually by reading *Detailed Statement* of each transaction. *frac* is calculated by shares offered in the offering and shares outstanding immediately after the offering. The former number is obtained from Wind's data screener "Primary Market", while the later using entry S_SHARE_TOTAL. I use S_FA_TA to obtain the value of *size*. I use S_FA_BPS to retrieve book value and S_VAL_MV to retrieve market value, so as to calculate *bm* by division. The value of *hitech* is determined manually by checking if an issuer belongs to the industries of Electronics, IT and Pharmaceutical and Biological Engineering. I use S_INFO_DLIST to retrieve the year when an issuer went public. The year of offering is available from data screener "Primary Market". Subtraction results in *age*. The value of *connection* is determined manually by reading *Detailed Statement* of each transaction. Finally I use S_HOLDER_PCT to retrieve the value of *lsper*. I use *roe* and *leverage* as control variables. *roe* is return on common equity the year before the issue, retrieved by S_FA_ROE, while *leverage* is calculated as debt over the sum of debt and equity. Debt-to-equity ratio is obtained by S_FA_RATIODE

Z-statistics are listed in the parentheses to the right of coefficients

Significance levels of 1, 5 and 10 % are denoted by ***, ** and * respectively

Table 3.6 shows results of Logit regressions of the largest shareholder's choice on independent variables.

Both signs of *lsper* and *abscon* are insignificantly different from zero, offering evidence to reject the *Anti-dilution Hypothesis*. The sign of *abscon* is even negative. I can conclude that the largest shareholder of a private offering firm does not care much about its ownership being reduced. The reason may be that in China it is well established in people's mind that a firm has a controlling shareholder and a slight change of ownership structure due to refinancing does not challenge the status of the controlling shareholder.

Two proxies of information asymmetry *size* and *age* are significantly larger than zero, thus help in explaining the controlling shareholder's choice. Their positive signs, however, are totally against the *Information Asymmetry Hypothesis*. It literally says the less severe information asymmetry on firm value, or the more the pubic knows the issuer, the more likely that the largest shareholder joins in the private offering. An interpretation of this result from another angle is, no matter how little outsiders know about an issuing firm, they are willing to contribute money in the firm's private refinancing campaign, so the controlling shareholder never has to worry about not being able to raise enough capital for the issuer in a private placement. As will be discussed later, this finding offers strong support to the *Tunneling Hypothesis* in Chap. 4.

In summary, both my hypotheses on the largest shareholder's choice of whether to buy shares in a firm's private offering are rejected: The largest shareholder does not worry about share dilution, neither does it have to purchase unwanted shares by institutional investors.

References

Claessens S, Djankov S, Fan JPH, Lang LHP (2000) Expropriation of minority shareholders in East Asia. CEI working paper series 2000-4, Hitotsubashi University, Japan

Cronqvist H, Nisson M (2005) The choice between rights offerings and private equity placements. J Financ Econ 78:375–407

Dyck IJA, Zingales L (2002) Private benefits of control: an international comparison. CEPR discussion paper no. 3177, CEPR

Eckbo BE, Masulis RW (1992) Adverse selection and the rights offer paradox. J Financ Econ 32:293–332

Gibson S, Safieddineb A, Sonti R (2004) Smart investments by smart money: evidence from seasoned equity offerings. J Financ Econ 72:581–604

Grinblatt M, Titman S (2002) Financial markets and corporate strategy. Irwen Professional

Hertzel M, Smith RL (1993) Market discounts and shareholder gains for placing equity privately. J Finance 48:459–485

Myers S, Majluf NS (1984) Corporate financing and investment decisions when firms have information that investors do not have. J Financ Econ 13:187–221

Tan RSK, Chng PL, Tong YH (2002) Private placements and rights issues in Singapore. Pac-Basin Finance J 10:29–54

Wruck KH (1989) Equity ownership concentration and firm value: evidence from private equity financings. J Financ Econ 23:3–28

Wu X, Wang Z, Yao J (2005) Understanding the positive announcement effects of private equity placements: new insights from Hong Kong data. Rev Finance 9:385–414

Chapter 4
Determinants of Private Placement Discount

Abstract In this chapter, I investigate how the offer discount is determined in a private placement in China. I find that China's private placements are sold to investors at an average discount of 24.83 %. Such discount does not reflect the largest shareholder or institutional investors increased monitoring efforts after the placement. There is also no consistent evidence that information costs explain the discount. In private placements where the largest shareholder buys shares, however, the discount is as high as 43.16 %.

Keywords Private placement • PIPE • Discount • Premium • Tunneling

4.1 Hypothesis Development

The *Monitoring Hypothesis* purports that, due to higher ownership concentration after the placement, purchasers of privately placed shares deserve a lower price than the prevailing market price. Here, higher ownership concentration is believed to induce more monitoring efforts from block-holders. In empirical studies such as Wruck (1989) and Hertzel and Smith (1993), ownership concentration is measured by adding up the ownership (measured in percentage) of large shareholders who possess 5 % or more of shares outstanding. While this measure may be suitable for the US case where listed firms generally do not have a distinguishable controlling shareholder, namely the largest shareholder, it serves to conceal much information on block holding in the case of China, where there is a controlling shareholder for a listed company. To capture the change of ownership concentration more precisely in China, I consider the increase of both the largest shareholder's holding and institutional investors' holding. Instead of claiming ambiguously that a more concentrated ownership structure leads to more stringent monitoring on firm management, I make a distinction between monitoring from the controlling shareholder and that from institutional investors. This results in the first two hypotheses on discount determination.

P. Song, *Private Placement of Public Equity in China*, SpringerBriefs in Finance,
DOI: 10.1007/978-3-642-55093-5_4,

H1: The larger the increase in the largest shareholder's holding, the larger the discount.

H2: The discount is higher for private placements after which there are institutional investors becoming top 10 shareholders of the firm.

Thus I have separated the *Monitoring Hypothesis* into two sub ones. H1 shows my interest in knowing if the largest shareholder does exert more monitoring and require that such efforts be compensated in the form of a discount. H2 says an institutional investor holding a substantial part of the issuer does play a role in helping (or monitoring) firm management and ask for a discount in return.

The *Information Cost Hypothesis*, being the most popular in the literature, purports that the discount is the cost of determining whether the private shares issuer has good prospects: The more difficult it is to evaluate firm value, the larger the discount should be; otherwise, purchasers of privately places shares are not able to get fair investment returns. This hypothesis is the most tested in relevant studies and I state it as my third hypothesis.

H3: The more severe the information asymmetry problem of an issuer, the larger the private placement discount.

As discussed, tunneling is a scarce subject in the literature on private placement. I strongly suspect the existence of tunneling in private placements, especially in China where corporate governance can be described as slack at best. Conjecturally, in a private placement the largest shareholder, who by definition controls the firm, can tunnel wealth from minor shareholders by many means. Three ways can be easily conceived. Firstly, if the largest shareholder would like to increase its percentage of holdings, it can initiate a private placement and inject cash or assets into the firm, even if the firm is not in need of extra capital at all. Secondly, a related party of the largest shareholder can inject cash/assets into the firm and profit from the firm's growth prospects while the firm already has adequate capital. Thirdly, even if the firm does need extra capital, the largest shareholder can ask for as many shares as possible in return for a given amount of cash/assets, or put in another way, ask for an unfairly high discount it does not deserve.

I conjecture that the third type of tunneling is present in private placements where the largest shareholder is the only purchaser or institutional investors join the largest shareholder as purchasers. In both cases, assuming that the largest shareholder is self-interested and rational, there is no reason why it would not like to increase holdings at a cost as low as possible. This does not mean that the largest shareholder can lower the offering price arbitrarily. On the one hand, I do admit that monitoring from minor investors matters in disciplining the largest shareholder's tunneling behavior. On the other hand, CSRC requires that the offering price should not be lower than the 20-day average stock price prior to the date when board of the issuer announces the placement. The bottom line of my argument is, given that the largest shareholder possesses presumably more information on the firm than minor investors and that it enjoys more control rights than cash flow rights, there is room for it to manipulate offering price in a private placement. This analysis holds even if institutional investors also participate in the placement.

On the one hand, it is in the largest shareholder's interest to collude with institutional investors, as long as the increase in institutional investors' holdings is not too high to threaten its controlling position. On the other hand, institutional investors are glad to have a purchase price as low as the largest shareholder has. This argument leads to my forth hypothesis.

H4: Other things equal, the discount in private placements in which the largest shareholder purchases shares is higher than the discount in private placements with no largest shareholder participation.

4.2 Sample Construction

In constructing the sample studied in this chapter, I start with the 670 private placement observations from 2007 to 2011 investigated in Chap. 3. From these observations, I first delete 59 private placements whose reference date for pricing is not the date on which the board makes the announcement, because the absence of a reference date indicates the private placement may not fully satisfy CSRC's regulatory requirements. I then drop 102 observations whose market transaction data for the 6 months prior to reference date are missing. Missing market transaction data usually indicates suspension of transaction, which is required for firms conceiving significant corporate events such as assets restructuring.[1] Finally I delete four observations of no share-holding data. After such filtration, I obtain a sample of 505 private placements conducted by 489 firms. There are two firms conducting three placements and 22 firms conducting two placements. Table 4.1 shows the whole process of sample construction. In the sample, controlling shareholders participate in 293 private placements, making 109 purchases by assets and 184 by cash.

Since the sample used in this chapter is not much different from the subsample of private placements in Chap. 3, I find it unnecessary to present sample statistics here.

4.3 Methodologies and Variable Construction

In this section, I make use of ordinary least square regression models to test the four hypotheses developed in Sect. 4.1.

The dependent variable is discount level, denoted $discount_i$ for observation i. There is no agreement as to how the discount should be calculated in the literature. In this study, I follow the mainstream (Wruck 1989; Hertzel and Smith 1993;

[1] A significant asset restructuring is required by CSRC to be accompanied by suspension of trading. Whether an activity is significant is determined by CSRC, so I am not able to offer a clear definition of significance. Generally, a significant restructuring activity includes, for example, a coal-mining company buying a mine whose value is bigger than the buying company's.

Table 4.1 Process of Sample Construction

	Private placements
Original observations	670
Delete: no benchmark price for discount calculation	59
Delete: no trading before board announcement	102
Delete: no share-holding data	4
Final sample	505
Largest shareholder participation	293
Purchase by assets	109
Purchase by cash	184

This table shows the data filtering process to reach the final sample I use in Chaps. 4 and 5. Benchmark Price means the minimum price the offering can be issued at, as required by CSRC. It is usually the average closing price of 20 trading days prior to board announcement. I delete 59 cases in which the benchmark price is not as CSRC requires. In 102 cases, trading on the issuer's stock was suspended for a long time before board announcement, so I delete these observations. I also drop four observations with missing share-holding data. For the final sample, I count the number of observations in which the controlling shareholder participates, purchases by assets and purchases by cash

Krishnamurthy et al. 2005) and define discount as the difference between the close price 10 days after *Detailed Statement* is published and the offering price, divided by the former, or

$$discount_i = \frac{i's\ closing\ price\ ten\ days\ after\ Detailed\ Statement - offering\ price}{i's\ closing\ price\ ten\ days\ after\ Detailed\ Statement} \tag{4.1}$$

Using the closing price 10 days after the final statement of the deal is announced allows me to incorporate market reactions to all information released in the placement process, including the board announcement, the shareholders' meeting announcement, the CRSC announcement, and the final announcement, and capture more precisely the implicit cost for shareholders in the process.[2]

To test H1 and H2, I employ three independent variables: $\Delta lsper$, $\Delta abscon$, and *topten*. For observation i, $\Delta lsper_i$ is the increase in the largest shareholder's percentage of holding after the placement. Note that $\Delta lsper_i$ is negative if the largest shareholder's holding decreases. $\Delta abscon_i$ is a dummy variable set to 1 if in observation i the largest shareholder becomes the absolute controller of the issuer after placement. Finally, if there is any institutional investor becoming a top-ten shareholder in observation i, then $topten_i = 1$; otherwise, $topten_i$ is set to 0. An institutional investor turning into a top-ten shareholder means its ownership of the issuer has increased dramatically. I hypothesize that if the largest shareholder obtains more shares through the

[2] In a previous draft of this book, I calculate discount using the stock price 10 days after board announcement, but not 10 days after final announcement. My previous approach fails to incorporate all information regarding a placement and yields an average discount level of 20 %. The new approach here yields a higher average discount level: 24.83 %.

Table 4.2 Variables and expected signs

Variable	Hypothesis related	Expected sign
discount	–	
Δlsper	Monitoring	+
Δabscon	Monitoring	+
topten	Monitoring	+
frac	Information cost	+
size	Information cost	−
bm	Information cost	−
hitech	Information cost	+
age	Information cost	−
lsp	Tunneling	+

This table shows variables used in testing my hypotheses and their expected signs in Chap. 4. *discount* is calculated as the offering price over the closing price 10 days after final announcement is made. *Δlsper* is the controlling shareholder's share of ownership after the offering subtracted by its ownership before the offering. *Δabscon* is calculated by subtracting *abscon* before the placement from *abscon* after the placement. *topten* is a dummy variable set to 1 if after the private placement, there is at least one participating institutional investor ranking top ten among all shareholders. *frac* is calculated as shares issued over shares outstanding after the issue. *size* is the log of total assets of the issuer prior to the offering, measured in billion Chines Yuan. *bm* is the book-to-market ratio widely used in literature. *hitech* is a dummy variable set to 1 if the issuer is in industries of Electronics, IT and Pharmaceutical and Biological Engineering. *age* is calculated by subtracting year of the offering by year the issuer went public. *lsp* is a dummy variable set to 1 if the largest shareholder of an issuer participates in the offering

placement, it would apply more monitoring on the management, and that if an institutional investor becomes as substantial as among top-ten investors, it would also strive to increase firm value by exerting more monitoring efforts. Thus, signs of *Δlsper*, *Δabscon* and *topten* are all expected to be positive.

To test H3, the same set of variables indicating information asymmetry as used in Chap. 3 are employed. They are *frac*, *size*, *bm*, *hitech* and *age*. More shares placed means more uncertainty regarding firm prospects. A high-technology firm placing a large amount of shares is considered to have a much uncertain firm value. Therefore, I expect the signs of *frac* and *hitech* to be positive. To the contrary, it entails less cost to determine the value of a listed firm of big market capitalization and book-to-market ratio. Information is also more readily available for firms that have been on the public market for a longer time. Thus the expected signs of *size*, *bm* and *age* are negative.

To test H4, I use dummy variable *lsp*, indicating presence and absence of the largest shareholder in a private placement. In Chap. 3, *lsp* acts as a dependent variable. Here, it becomes an independent variable. I have argued that the largest shareholder is being rational in setting a higher discount (and consequently lower offering price) than it deserves so that it can increase its holding as much as possible with a given amount of capital contribution, so the sign of *lsp* is expected to be positive.

Table 4.2 exhibits definitions and expected signs of variables.

4.4 Empirical Tests

4.4.1 Descriptive Statistics and Mean-Difference Analysis

I present descriptive statistics of my sample in Panel A of Table 4.3.

Panel A reveals that on average, participants of a private placement enjoy a discount as high as 24.83 %. This is higher than the 20.14 % discount level documented by Hertzel and Smith (1993) for the US, the 10.2 % discount level documented by Anderson et al. (2006) for New Zealand, and the 5.15 % discount in Hong Kong documented by Wu et al. (2005). Tan et al. (2002) even find most private placements are carried out at a premium in Singapore. Thus it is safe to claim that in China, participants of a private placement enjoy a higher offering discount than their foreign counterparts. It's striking that the highest discount observed is 535 %.

A typical controlling shareholder's ownership increases by 1.44 % after the placement. Four percent of controlling shareholders become the absolute controller via the offering. In 24 % of all observations, there is at least one institutional investor becoming a top-ten shareholder. In my sample, the largest shareholder participates in 47 % of transactions; institutional investors are the only purchasers in 53 % of private placements. This confirms consistency of the sample used in Chap. 3 and this chapter: The controlling shareholder participates in about half of all transactions.

In Panel B, I conduct rank tests and calculate the difference between the mean of dependent variable for different subsamples. For each continuous independent variable, I rank its value and divide observations into three groups according to their ranking. I then calculate the mean of discount for each subgroup of observations. For each dummy variable, I simply calculate the mean discount for observations whose variable value is 1 and these of value 0.

p-values for the three variables indicating change of ownership concentration tell that these variables may not hold explanatory power for discount. It is also clear that *frac*, *bm* and *hitech* may help explain discount. Finally, it is shown that the average discount of private placements with largest shareholder presence is as high as 43.61 %, while in private placements where institutional investors are the only purchaser the discount is merely 8.80 %. The controlling shareholder enjoys an extra discount of 34.81 % in private offerings.

4.4.2 Regression Analysis

Table 4.4 displays results of my regression analysis.

The coefficient of *topten* is insignificant in all regressions, indicating the failure of H3; institutional investors' cost in monitoring firm management is not compensated in the form of discount. The variable $\Delta lsper$ is significantly different from zero when it acts as the only independent variable, but its significance elapses

Table 4.3 Descriptive statistics, rank tests and mean analysis

Variable	Mean	Median	Std error	Maximum	Minimum
Panel A: Descriptive statistics					
discount (%)	24.83	8.50	80.8	535	−76.54
Δlsper (%)	1.44	−2.12	13	64.72	−24.3
Δabscon	0.04	0	0.42	1	−1
topten	0.24	0	0.43	1	0
frac (%)	17.10	11.42	15	79.30	0.89
size	9.60	9.46	0.56	11.36	8.37
bm	0.28	0.18	0.28	3.55	−0.03
hitech	0.19	0	0.39	1	0
age	8.20	8	3.90	16	1
lsp	0.47	0	0.5	1	0

(continued)

Table 4.3 (continued)

Variable	Range of value	Discount Mean (%)	Discount p-value	Number of observations
Panel B: Rank test and mean analysis				
Δlsper (%)	(−24.3, −4.45)	13.10	0.17	168
	(−4.44, 0.53)	7		168
	(0.54, 67.42)	59.22		169
Δabscon	−1	11.59	0.31	168
	0	27.60		168
	1	13.70		169
topten	0	24.37	0.54	399
	1	26.34		106
frac	(0.01, 0.08)	−19.90	0.03	168
	(0.08, 0.17)	7.92		168
	(0.17, 0.79)	83.8		169
size	(8.36, 9.31)	19	0.23	168
	(9.31, 9.71)	36.3		168
	(9.71, 11.36)	19		169
bm	(−0.03, 0.14)	52	0.00	168
	(0.14, 0.23)	15		168
	(0.23, 3.54)	8		169
hitech	0	23	0.07	402
	1	31		103

(continued)

Table 4.3 (continued)

Variable	Range of value	Discount		Number of observations
		Mean (%)	*p*-value	
age	(1, 5)	1.3	0.75	168
	(6, 11)	33.40		168
	(12, 16)	35.17		169
lsp	0	8.80	0.00	212
	1	43.61		293

This table shows descriptive statistics for private placements. Rank tests and mean-difference analysis are conducted in Panel B. The value of *discount* is calculated as offering price divided by closing price 10 days after final announcement. The former figure is obtained from data screener "Primary Market". The later is from entry S_VAL_MV. *Δlsper* is the result of subtracting the controlling shareholder's percentage of holding before placement from the holding after. Holding data is collected using S_HOLDER_PCT. *frac* is calculated by shares offered in the offering and shares outstanding immediately after the offering. The former number is obtained from Wind's data screener "Primary Market", while the later using entry S_SHARE_TOTAL. I use S_FA_TA to obtain the value of *size*. I use S_FA_BPS to retrieve book value and S_VAL_MV to retrieve market value, so as to calculate *bm* by division. The value of *hitech* is determined manually by checking if an issuer belongs to the industries of Electronics, IT and Pharmaceutical and Biological Engineering. I use S_INFO_DLIST to retrieve the year when an issuer went public. The year of offering is available from data screener "Primary Market". Subtraction results in *age*. *lsp* is also from data screener "Primary Market"

Table 4.4 Regression results on discount

	1	2	3	4	5	6	7	8
Intercept	−0.2624***	−0.1470	0.0512	−0.1413	−0.4297	0.3223**	0.2797**	−0.2250
	(−3.38)	(−1.30)	(0.39)	(−0.50)	(−0.50)	(3.84)	(2.10)	(−0.25)
Δlsper						0.0214***	0.0212	0.0043
						(4.92)	(0.67)	(0.98)
Δabscon							0.0437	0.1016
							(0.32)	(0.93)
topten							−0.0694	−0.0743
							(−0.51)	(−0.69)
frac	3.5407***	3.5955***		3.6420***	3.6929***			3.5323***
	(11.75)	(11.71)		(12.33)	(12.06)			(10.49)
size					0.0306			0.0134
					(0.31)			(0.13)
bm	−0.4598***	−0.4988***		−0.4925***	−0.4847***			−0.4958***
	(−2.89)	(−3.08)		(−3.06)	(−2.84)			(−2.89)
hitech					0.1396			0.1566
					(1.21)			(1.33)
age					−0.0062			−0.0055
					(−0.51)			(−0.44)
lsp	0.3540***	0.3569***	0.3307**					0.335***
	(2.82)	(2.57)	(2.73)					(3.00)
roe		−0.3596	−0.3530	−0.3456	−0.3770	−0.7568*	−0.8313*	−0.5264
		(−0.99)	(−0.74)	(−0.96)	(−0.98)	(−1.62)	(−1.72)	(−1.30)

(continued)

Table 4.4 (continued)

	1	2	3	4	5	6	7	8
leverage		−0.2203	0.2506	−0.1982	−0.1639		0.1829	−0.1804
		(−1.01)	(0.39)	(−0.92)	(−0.66)		(0.66)	(−0.72)
Year control	Yes	Yes	Yes	Yes	Yes	Yes	Yes	Yes
F statistic	53.04	42.07	23.33	40.16	23.03	12.19	4.91	14.78
ADJ R^2	0.4563	0.4587	0.3366	0.4599	0.4559	0.1074	0.1205	0.4517
Observations	185	185	185	185	185	185	185	185

This table shows OLS regression results of discount on various independent variables. The value of *discount* is calculated as closing price 10 days after final announcement divided by offering price, minus 1. The former figure is obtained from data screener "Primary Market". The later is from entry S_DQ_CLOSE. *Δlsper* is the result of subtracting the controlling shareholder's percentage of holding before placement from the holding after. Holding data is collected via S_HOLDER_PCT. *frac* is calculated by shares offered in the offering and shares outstanding immediately after the offering. The former number is obtained from Wind's data screener "Primary Market", while the later using entry S_SHARE_TOTAL. I use S_FA_TA to obtain the value of *size.* I use S_FA_BPS to retrieve book value and S_VAL_MV to retrieve market value, so as to calculate *bm* by division. The value of *hitech* is determined manually by checking if an issuer belongs to the industries of Electronics, IT and Pharmaceutical and Biological Engineering. I use S_INFO_DLIST to retrieve the year when an issuer went public. The year of offering is available from data screener "Primary Market". Subtraction results in *age*. *lsp* is also from data screener "Primary Market". *roe* is return on common equity and obtained via S_FA_ROE. *leverage* is debt over the sum of debt and equity and can be calculated from debt-to-equity ratio, which is retrieved by S_FA_RATIODE

T-statistics are listed in the parentheses below or to the right of coefficients

Significance levels of 1 %, 5 % and 10 % are denoted by ***, ** and * respectively

when I include other independent variables. It seems that the discount does not reflect the largest shareholder's increased monitoring efforts either. This finding is opposite to Wruck (1989) and Hertzel and Smith (1993)'s proposition that monitoring is compensated in the US, but offers support to Wu et al. (2005)'s assertion that ownership structure has nothing to do with discount determination in Hong Kong. Failure of the *Monitoring Hypothesis* may due to that in both China and Hong Kong, there is usually a controlling shareholder for a listed firm, while in the US firm ownership is much more scattered.

Among proxies of information asymmetry, *frac* and *bm* are significantly different from zero both at 1 % level. In the previous section, *hitech* showed the possibility of being significant, but regression analysis excludes it as a significant explanatory variable. It seems that purchasers of privately placed shares indeed are compensated for their costs in determining firm value. This is extended evidence for what Hertzel and Smith (1993) have proposed in their prominent work.

As expected in my rank tests, *lsp* is significantly positive in all regressions at 1 % level. Its coefficient is around 34 %, indicating that as long as the largest shareholder purchases shares in a private offering, the offering price is lower by 34 %. The largest shareholder indeed is enjoying a much lower offering price, other things being equal. It seems that institutional investors had better participate in private placements together with the largest shareholder, but not alone. The largest shareholder may argue that it deserves a higher discount because institutional investors are not contributing enough capital to the issuer. However, I have proved in the previous chapter that no matter how severe information asymmetry regarding the issuer's true value is, there are always institutional investors willing to participate in the private offering. The largest shareholder may also claim that the extra discount is a form of compensation for long-run weak performance of the issuer's stock. I will reject this possibility in Chap. 6. In summary, the *Tunneling Hypothesis* cannot be rejected. This is an important contribution to the literature: Using China's unique private placement dataset, I show that the controlling shareholder tunnels wealth from small shareholders to itself through private placement. Private placement, while being a way of raising additional capital for the firm, also serves as a channel of tunneling when the largest shareholder is present.

4.5 Robustness Check

The offering price floor required by CSRC provides a unique opportunity to check if my findings are robust. In this section, I investigate offering price from another perspective rather than discount: The premium of offering price over the minimum price, or

$$premium_i = \frac{i's\ offer\ price - minimum\ price\ for\ i}{minimum\ price\ for\ i} \tag{4.2}$$

Conceivably, in a private placement the largest shareholder would like as low a premium as possible, just as it pursues the highest possible discount. A correlation

Table 4.5 Regression results on premium

	1	2	3	4	5	6	7
Intercept	0.3447***	0.3113***	0.3180***	0.2951***	1.0641	0.2409***	0.9719**
	(5.32)	(5.27)	(5.61)	(5.03)	(2.27)	(4.05)	(1.98)
Δlsper						−0.0061 (0.69)	−0.0022 (−0.91)
Δabscon						−0.0149 (−0.24)	0.0028 (0.05)
topten						0.0029 (0.05)	−0.0122 (−0.21)
frac	−0.6712***	−0.6469***		−0.7250***	−0.7820***		−0.6766***
	(−4.09)	(−3.94)		(−4.56)	(−4.54)		(−3.67)
size					−0.0829 (−1.58)		−0.0745 (−1.34)
bm					−0.0500 (−0.54)		−0.0463 (−0.50)
hitech	0.2016***	0.2057***		0.2175***	0.2162***		0.2088***
	(3.28)	(3.33)		(3.53)	(3.47)		(3.29)
age					0.0005 (0.08)		0.0013 (0.21)
lsp	−0.3993**	−0.3893**	−0.3621**				−0.4546***
	(−3.86)	(−3.75)	(−3.12)				(−3.37)
roe		0.2487 (1.29)	0.2897 (1.41)	0.2277 (1.18)	0.3130 (1.51)	0.4034* (1.87)	0.3622** (1.65)
leverage		−0.0323	−0.1681	−0.0640	0.0263	−0.1837	0.0471
		(−0.27)	(−1.37)	(−0.54)	(0.20)	(−1.49)	(0.72)
Year control	Yes	Yes	Yes	Yes	Yes	Yes	Yes
F statistic	24.19	18.80	15.10	20.11	12.37	2.86	14.28
Adj R^2	0.1755	0.1748	0.1627	0.1753	0.1711	0.0482	0.1655
Observations	185	185	185	185	185	185	185

This table shows OLS regression results of premium on various independent variables. The value of *premium* is calculated as offering price divided by minimum price, minus 1. Both figures are obtained from data screener "Primary Market". *Δlsper* is the result of subtracting the controlling shareholder's percentage of holding before placement from the holding after. Holding data is collected vis S_HOLDER_PCT. *frac* is calculated by shares offered in the offering and shares outstanding immediately after the offering. The former number is obtained from Wind's data screener "Primary Market", while the later using entry S_SHARE_TOTAL. I use S_FA_TA to obtain the value of *size.* I use S_FA_BPS to retrieve book value and S_VAL_MV to retrieve market value, so as to calculate *bm* by division. The value of *hitech* is determined manually by checking if an issuer belongs to the industries of Electronics, IT and Pharmaceutical and Biological Engineering. I use S_INFO_DLIST to retrieve the year when an issuer went public. The year of offering is available from data screener "Primary Market". Subtraction results in *age*. *lsp* is also from data screener "Primary Market". *roe* is return on common equity and obtained via S_FA_ROE. *leverage* is debt over the sum of debt and equity and can be calculated from debt-to-equity ratio, which is retrieved by S_FA_RATIODE

T-statistics are listed in the parentheses below or to the right of coefficients

Significance levels of 1 %, 5 % and 10 % are denoted by ***, ** and * respectively

of −1 between discount and premium would render regressions using premium as the dependent variable useless. Fortunately, my calculation shows that the premium is not perfectly negatively correlated with discount, so looking into the relationship between premium and independent variables is worth efforts: If coefficients of independent variables are of opposite signs to the signs found in Sect. 3.4.3, then it is fair to claim that my regressions pass the robustness check.

Table 4.5 shows results from regressions of the premium on the same set of independent variables used in Sect. 3.4.3.

Again, variables indicating changes of ownership concentration are not significantly different from zero. *Monitoring Hypothesis* fails. The information proxy *bm* is no longer a good explanatory variable for premium as it is for discount. Instead, *hitech* is significant in explaining offering premium. Its sign is positive, indicating that a high-technology issuer offers its shares at a higher premium over price floor, consistent with the *Information Cost Hypothesis.*

The sign of *lsp* is significantly negative at 1 % level in one regression and at 5 % level in three regressions. This shows, when the largest shareholder participates in a private placement, the premium over floor price is lower by around 4 %, evidence that the largest shareholder is rationally tunneling wealth from other shareholders.

In conclusion, both regressions on discount and premium reject the *Monitoring Hypothesis*. Private shares purchasers are not compensated for more monitoring efforts after the placement, if there is any more monitoring at all. The *Information Cost Hypothesis* is supported: The more difficult it is to determine firm value, the lower the offering price to compensate purchasers. Finally, statistically the presence of the controlling shareholder means an offering discount higher by 34 %. I posit that this is evidence of the largest shareholder tunneling wealth from other shareholders, which is rational of the largest shareholder but undesirable for other shareholders. Institutional investors joining the controlling shareholder in a private placement also enjoy the extra discount, but whether they are colluding with the controlling shareholder is beyond scope of this book.

References

Anderson HD, Rose LC, Cahan SF (2006) Differential shareholder wealth and volume effects surrounding private equity placements in New Zealand. Pac Basin Finan J 14:367–395

Hertzel M, Smith RL (1993) Market discounts and shareholder gains for placing equity privately. J Finan 48:459–485

Krishnamurthy S, Spindt P, Subramaniam V, Woidtke T (2005) Does investor identity matter in equity issues? Evidence from private placements. J Finan Intermediation 14:210–238

Tan RSK, Chng PL, Tong YH (2002) Private placements and rights issues in Singapore. Pac Basin Finan J 10:29–54

Wruck KH (1989) Equity ownership concentration and firm value: evidence from private equity financings. J Finan Econ 23:3–28

Wu X, Wang Z, Yao J (2005) Understanding the positive announcement effects of private equity placements: New insights from Hong Kong data. Rev Finan 9:385–414

Chapter 5
Announcement Effect

Abstract In this chapter, I calculate announcement period abnormal return of private placements. The abnormal return is significantly positive. Again, increased monitoring from the largest shareholder or big institutional investors does not explain the positivity. There is mixed evidence whether reduction of information asymmetry causes positive announcement-period abnormal return and inadequate evidence whether more credible information leads to higher market reaction.

Keywords Private placement • PIPE • Market reaction • Announcement-period abnormal return • Cumulative abnormal return

In this chapter, I first calculate the short-term abnormal return to private shares issuers around the announcement and then analyze factors that help explain the excess return. Announcement effects of corporate actions or other substantial changes are extensively studied in the finance literature. For private placements, this is perhaps the most investigated aspect. The setting in China complicates my study in that, as shown in Chap. 1, there are several announcements made in the process of a private placement. At first, board of a firm announces its plan to raise additional capital through private offering. Later the shareholders' meeting approves the campaign and makes a second announcement. The firm then submits an application to CSRC, who, upon approval of the application, makes the third announcement. Finally, the forth announcement in the form of *Detailed Statement* is publicized when all transactions are settled. Correspondingly, there are four announcement effects.

However and fortunately, information flow through the process reduces announcement effects of concern to two: Around the board announcement and around the publication of *Detailed Statement*. Public investors learn about the firm's intention to raise extra capital via private placement through the first announcement and about details of the transaction through the last. The second and the third announcements convey no new information to investors. In this sense, I only need to calculate two short-term abnormal returns. Later in this chapter, it will be shown that information on the transaction is mostly released to the public before the final announcement.

P. Song, *Private Placement of Public Equity in China*, SpringerBriefs in Finance,
DOI: 10.1007/978-3-642-55093-5_5, © The Author(s) 2014

These two announcement effects reflect investors' responses to different sets of information. Initially when the board makes an announcement, it tells nothing more than the fact that the firm is trying to offer shares privately, so investors' reaction can only be related to existing firm attributes which include firm size, book-to-market ratio, whether the firm is a high-technology one, etc. At last when *Detailed Statement* is published, various aspects of the transaction are revealed, and investors now respond to a lot more information: Whether the largest shareholder purchases shares, how many institutional investors arc involved, how many shares are placed, etc. In this regard, I will relate the two announcement effects to two different sets of independent variables.

5.1 Hypothesis Development

The literature has documented positive announcement effects for private placements in almost all countries.[1] Although through such an offering, more shares of a stock will be added to the market (the *Price Pressure Effect*) and wealth is regarded to be transferred from shareholders to lenders (the *Wealth Transfer Effect*), so that downward pressure is imposed on the price of the stock, I still expect the abnormal return around a private placement announcement to be positive. My first hypothesis says,

H1: *The announcement effect of a private placement in China is positive.*

The *Monitoring Effect* purports that, due to higher ownership concentration after the placement, firm management will be better monitored and investors will react favorably to this change. As discussed in Chap. 4, higher ownership concentration results from the change of shareholdings for two types of investors. On the one hand, the largest shareholder may hold more of the firm by purchasing enough shares in the placement. On the other hand, some institutional investors may gain substantial control rights after participating in the placement. Instead of claiming vaguely that a more concentrated ownership structure leads to more stringent monitoring on firm management, I make a distinction between monitoring from the largest shareholder and that from institutional investors. This results in two hypotheses.

H2: *The larger the increase in the largest shareholder's holding, the larger the announcement effect.*

H3: *The announcement effect is higher for private placements after which there are institutional investors becoming top 10 shareholders of the firm.*

Thus I have separated the *Monitoring Effect* into two sub ones. H1 shows my interest in knowing if the market believes that the largest shareholder will exert

[1] An exception is Tan et al. (2002). They document premium but not discount in private offerings, and find the market reaction to a private offering announcement to be negative in Singapore. The legal setting of private placement is different in Singapore from other countries, so their study does not ruin findings in other studies on private placement.

more monitoring efforts after an increase in its holding. H2 says a substantial institutional investor does give public investors the impression that firm management will be better disciplined.

The *Signaling Effect*, being the most popular in the literature, posits that the market reacts to more information released about the issuer: The more favorable the information on firm value is, the higher the market reaction. In a private placement, two conditions can be defined as generating favorable information. Firstly, more uncertainty on firm value prior to the offering means that new information is more favorable to public investors: More information means less uncertainty. Secondly, more credible information is also more favorable. I address these two lines with two hypotheses.

H4: *The more severe the information asymmetry problem of the issuer, the larger the announcement effect.*

H5: *The announcement effect is increasing in credibility of the signal sent through private placements.*

In Sect. 5.3, I will also test *Price Pressure Effect* and *Wealth Transfer Effect* that are discussed previously.

5.2 Methodologies and Variable Construction

In this section, I test Hypothesis 1 by calculating CAR (cumulative abnormal return), and apply ordinary least square regression models to the same sample as used in Chap. 4 to test if various effects of concern really hold.

The dependent variable is the cumulative abnormal return of an issuer's stock around announcements. In this study, I use the market model to estimate benchmark returns. Firstly, using market return $R_{m,t}$ and stock return $R_{i,t}$ at window $[-200, -60]$, I get observation i's α and β estimates in the market model, namely $\hat{\alpha}_i$ and $\hat{\beta}_i$. The abnormal return for i at day t is

$$AR_{i,t} = R_{i,t} - (\hat{\alpha}_i + \hat{\beta}_i R_{m,t}) \quad (5.1)$$

For each day t, I then calculate the average abnormal return of all observations as

$$AAR_t = \frac{\sum_{i=1}^{N} AR_{i,t}}{N} \quad (5.2)$$

The cumulative abnormal return for observation i between day t_1 and t_2 is calculated as $CAR_i[t_1, t_2] = \sum_{t_1}^{t_2} AR_{i,t}$. The average cumulative return for all observations between t_1 and t_2 follows as $CAR[t_1, t_2] = \sum_{i=1}^{N} CAR_i[t_1, t_2]/N$.

Extant studies on private placements have defined various windows [t_1, t_2] as the announcement period. To facilitate comparisons with most of them, I follow Wruck (1989) and Hertzel and Smith (1993) and set [t_1, t_2] to [−3, 0], namely the CAR from 3 days before an announcement to the announcement date. As discussed in the introduction, two CARs are calculated for each observation in the sample, one around board announcement and the other around publication of the final *Detailed Statement*. I denote the former as $CAR_{B,i}[-3, 0]$, where B stands for Board, and the latter as $CAR_{F,i}[-3, 0]$, where F stands for Final.

I test H1 by checking if calculated CAR is bigger than 0 in one-sided tests.

To test H2 and H3, I employ dependent variable $CAR_{F,i}[-3, 0]$ and three independent variables: $\Delta lsper$, $\Delta abscon$, and *topten*. I ignore $CAR_{B,i}[-3, 0]$ here because no information of ownership change is revealed to the public at board announcement. I hypothesize that if the largest shareholder obtains more shares through the placement, public investors will believe that it would apply more monitoring on the management, and that if an institutional investor becomes as substantial as among the top ten investors, it sends the market a signal that it would strive to increase firm value by exerting more monitoring efforts. Thus, signs of $\Delta lsper$, $\Delta abscon$ and *topten* are all expected to be positive.

To test H4, the same set of variables indicating information asymmetry as used in Chaps. 3 and 4 are employed. They are *frac*, *size*, *bm*, *hitech* and *age*. At board announcement, *size*, *bm*, *hitech* and *age* are known publicly, so I associate these independent variables with $CAR_{B,i}[-3, 0]$. Variable *frac* is not available to the public until *Detailed Statement* is in place, so I associate it with $CAR_{F,i}[-3, 0]$. I expect the signs of *frac* and *hitech* to be positive. To the contrary, the expected signs of *size*, *bm* and *age* are negative.

To test H5, I use dependent variable $CAR_F[-3, 0]$ and independent variable *noin*, which stands for the number of institutional investors purchasing shares in a private placement. I regard *noin* as a good but not perfect proxy for credibility of the firm value signal sent through *Detailed Statement*. A better proxy should be the number of institutional investors bidding for shares in a private placement. Only a limited number of *Detailed Statements* present the number of share bidders. Fortunately, in these cases the number of bidders is closely correlated to the number of institutional investors successfully obtaining allotments. The sign of *noin* is expected to be positive: The more institutional investors purchasing shares in a placement, the higher the market reaction.

Following Anderson et al. (2006), I also test the *Price Pressure Effect* and the *Wealth Transfer Effect* by using variables *liq* and Δde respectively. The higher the liquidity, the lower the private pressure. So I expect the sign of *liq* to be positive. A larger decrease in debt-to-equity ratio means more wealth is transferred from shareholders to debt-holders, so I assume the sign of Δde will be positive.

Table 5.1 exhibits definitions and expected signs of variables.

5.3 Empirical Tests

5.3.1 Descriptive Statistics and Mean-Difference Analysis

Firstly I present the time series of average abnormal returns in Fig. 5.1. AARs around both board announcement and final announcement exhibit a rising tendency around day 0. AAR around board announcement reaches the peak at day -1,

Table 5.1 Variables and expected signs

Variable	Hypothesis related	Expected sign
$\Delta lsper$	Monitoring	+
$\Delta abscon$	Monitoring	+
topten	Monitoring	+
frac	Signaling	+
size	Signaling	−
bm	Signaling	−
hitech	Signaling	+
age	Signaling	−
noin	Signaling	+
liq	Price pressure	−
Δde	Wealth transfer	+

This table shows variables used in testing my hypotheses and their expected signs in Chap. 5. $\Delta lsper$ is the controlling shareholder's share of ownership after the offering subtracted by its ownership prior to the offering. $\Delta abscon$ is calculated by subtracting *abscon* before the placement from *abscon* after the placement. *topten* is a dummy variable set to 1 if after the private placement, there is at least one participating institutional investor ranking top ten among all shareholders. *frac* is calculated as shares issued over shares outstanding immediately after the issue. *size* is the log of total assets of the issuer prior to the offering, measured in billion Chines Yuan. *bm* is the book-to-market ratio widely used in literature. *hitech* is a dummy variable set to 1 if the issuer is in industries of Electronics, IT and Pharmaceutical and Biological Engineering. *age* is calculated by subtracting year of the offering by year the issuer went public. *noin* is the number of institutional investors participating in a private placement. *liq* stands for liquidity and is calculated as average trading volume of 30 trading days prior to board announcement over total shares outstanding before board announcement. Δde is the decrease in debt-to-equity ratio after the placement

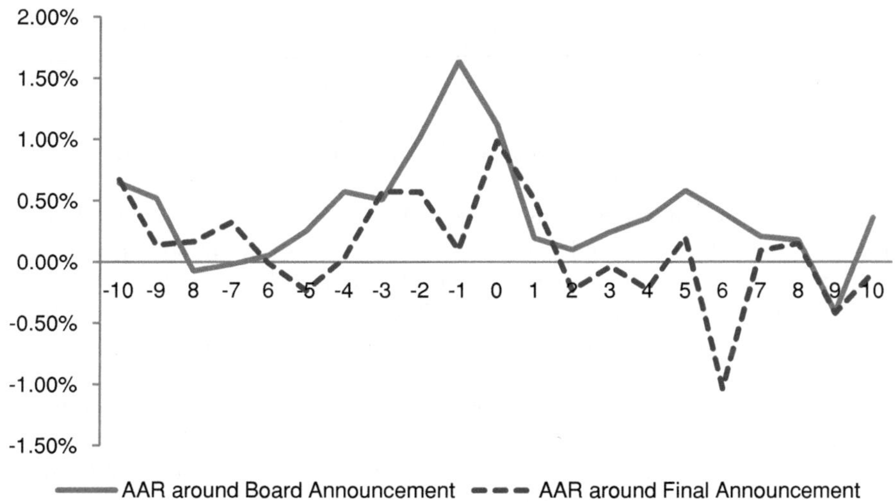

Fig. 5.1 Time Series of AARs. This figure shows average abnormal returns of all observations from 10 days before the announcement to 10 days after. The *solid line* refers to AARs around board announcement, while the *dotted line* refers to AARs around final announcement. Data on stock price are obtained from Wind with S_DQ_CLOSE

Table 5.2 CARs

	CAR (%)	*p*-value
Panel A: CAR_B		
[−3, 0]	4.30	0.03
[−5, 0]	5.73	0.00
Panel B: CAR_F		
[−3, 0]	2.23	0.07
[−5, 0]	1.14	0.15

This table shows average cumulative abnormal returns around the board announcement and final announcement. Data on stock price are obtained from Wind with S_DQ_CLOSE

while AAR around final announcement reaches its maximum at day 0. After day 2, both AARs become flat around 0.

I present my calculation of cumulative abnormal returns in Table. 5.2. Panel A displays the CAR of board announcement. The four-day CAR for [−3, 0] is 4.30 %, significantly positive at level 3 %. This is larger than what Hertzel and Smith (1993) find for the US, or 1.72 %. The abnormal return is robust in that the six-day CAR for [−5, 0] is 5.73 % and even more significant. Panel B displays the CAR of final announcement. The four-day CAR for [−3, 0] is 2.23 %, lower than its board-announcement counterpart but still significantly positive at 7 % level and higher than the 1.72 % announcement effect in the US (Hertzel and Smith 1993). To check its robustness, I also calculate for the six-day window. CAR [−5, 0] is 1.14 %, not different from zero at 10 % significance level, but different from zero at 15 % level. My calculation shows the abnormal return around final announcement, although statistically positive, is less prominent than that around board announcement. A possible explanation for such decrease in significance is information has been dispersed along the way a private placement is carried out. However, this is enough evidence that the announcement effect of a private placement is positive; the null hypothesis that the announcement effect of a private placement is zero is rejected. This adds to the popular finding that announcement effect of a private placement is positive (Hertzel and Smith 1993; Anderson et al. 2006; and others).

I am using the same sample as in Chap. 4, so it is unnecessary to list descriptive statistics for most of independent variables. However, variable *noin* is new to Chap. 5. According to my calculation, on average, there are six institutional investors in a private placement. Since CSRC requires that there should be at most ten institutional investors in a private offering, the maximum of *noin* in my sample is 10.

In Table 5.3, I calculate the difference between the mean of CAR for subsamples and conduct rank tests. As I do in Chap. 4, I calculate two means of CAR for independent variables that are dummies, and calculate three means of CAR for independent variables that are continuous. Panel A shows two independent variables, *size* and *hitech*, may be useful in explaining CAR around board announcement. In Panel B, $\Delta lsper$, *size* and *hitech* appear to be significant explanatory variables for the abnormal return around final announcement.

Table 5.3 Rank tests and mean analysis

Variable	Range of value	Discount Mean (%)	Discount *p*-value	Number of observations
Panel A: Rank test for CAR_B				
size	(8.37, 9.26)	5.67	0.08	168
	(9.26, 9.60)	3.73		168
	(9.61, 11.36)	3.66		169
bm	(–0.01, 0.16)	5.62	0.33	168
	(0.16, 0.27)	6.33		168
	(0.27, 0.69)	0.43		169
hitech	0	3.47	0.00	402
	1	7.39		103
age	(1, 5)	1.59	0.28	168
	(6, 9)	6.52		168
	(10, 16)	4.76		169
Panel B: Rank test for CAR_F				
$\Delta lsper$	(–23.23 %, –5.33 %)	2.32	0.08	168
	(–5.28 %, –2.27 %)	1.40		168
	(–2.27 %, 54.4 %)	2.90		169
$\Delta abscon$	–1	4.2	0.56	59
	0	2.18		406
	1	–1.8		42
topten	0	1.69	0.11	337
	1	2.54		168
frac	(0.01, 0.07)	1.39	0.26	168
	(0.07, 0.13)	2.72		168
	(0.13, 0.46)	2.60		169
size	(8.37, 9.29)	3.57	0.09	168
	(9.30, 9.62)	1.9		168
	(9.63, 11.36)	1.3		169

(continued)

Table 5.3 (continued)

Variable	Range of value	Discount		Number of observations
		Mean (%)	*p*-value	
bm	(−0.01, 0.16)	4.37	0.37	168
	(0.16, 0.26)	1.03		168
	(0.26, 0.69)	1.3		169
hitech	0	2.31	0.09	402
	1	1.90		103
age	(1, 5)	3.49	0.68	169
	(6, 9)	0.48		168
	(9, 16)	2.55		168
noin	(0, 5)	1.71	0.15	168
	(6, 8)	2.54		169
	(9, 10)	2.23		168
liq	(0, 0.007)	1.91	0.13	168
	(0.008, 0.015)	2.31		168
	(0.016, 0.019)	2.31		169
Δde	(−143%, −36%)	3.18	0.65	168
	(−36%, 0)	1.39		168
	(0, 628%)	2.67		169

This table shows rank tests and mean-difference analysis on announcement-period abnormal return. $\Delta lsper$ is the result of subtracting the controlling shareholder's percentage of holding before placement from the holding after. Holding data is collected via S_HOLDER_PCT. *frac* is calculated by shares offered in the offering and shares outstanding immediately after the offering. The former number is obtained from Wind's data screener "Primary Market", while the later using entry S_SHARE_TOTAL. I use S_FA_TA to obtain the value of *size*. I use S_FA_BPS to retrieve book value and S_VAL_MV to retrieve market value, so as to calculate *bm* by division. The value of *hitech* is determined manually by checking if an issuer belongs to the industries of Electronics, IT and Pharmaceutical and Biological Engineering. I use S_INFO_DLIST to retrieve the year when an issuer went public. The year of offering is available from data screener "Primary Market". Subtraction results in *age*. *noin* is obtained manually from *Detailed Statement*. *liq* is calculated as average trading volume of 30 trading days prior to board announcement over total shares outstanding before board announcement. Trading volume is retrieved using S_DQ_VOLUME. Δde is the decrease in debt-to-equity ratio after the placement. Debt-to-equity ratio is obtained using S_FA_RATIODE

Table 5.4 Regression results on CAR_B

	1	2	3	4
Intercept	0.04260	0.1786	0.011	0.0857
	(1.66)	(1.24)	(0.08)	(0.58)
size		−0.0149	0.0042	0.0048
		(−0.90)	(0.27)	(−0.3)
bm	−0.1709***		−0.1559***	−0.1642***
	(−2.95)		(−3.09)	(−2.70)
hitech	0.0364**		0.0327*	0.0363**
	(2.07)		(1.90)	(2.03)
age	0.0037**		0.0038**	0.0040**
	(2.07)		(2.03)	(2.06)
roe	−0.1018	−0.0978		−0.1031
	(−1.25)	(−1.14)		(1.26)
leverage	0.0360	0.0043		0.0856
	(0.96)	(1.10)		(0.58)
Year control	Yes	Yes	Yes	Yes
F statistic	4.03	1.05	4.73	3.35
Adj R^2	0.1114	0.0011	0.1060	0.1044
Observations	505	505	505	505

This table shows OLS regression results of CAR_B on various independent variables. I use S_FA_TA to obtain the value of *size*. I use S_FA_BPS to retrieve book value and S_VAL_MV to retrieve market value, so as to calculate *bm* by division. The value of *hitech* is determined manually by checking if an issuer belongs to the industries of Electronics, IT and Pharmaceutical and Biological Engineering. I use S_INFO_DLIST to retrieve the year when an issuer went public. The year of offering is available from data screener "Primary Market". Subtraction results in *age*. *lsp* is also from data screener "Primary Market". *roe* is return on common equity and obtained via S_FA_ROE. *leverage* is debt over the sum of debt and equity and can be calculated from debt-to-equity ratio, which is retrieved by S_FA_RATIODE

T-statistics are listed in the parentheses below coefficients

Significance levels of 1, 5 and 10 % are denoted by ***, ** and * respectively

5.3.2 Regression Analysis

Tables 5.4 and 5.5 display results of my regression analysis on both board announcement and final announcement CARs.

As rank tests promise, *hitech* significantly explains CAR around board announcement with a positive sign. A high-technology issuer generally experiences larger announcement-period abnormal return. Variable *size* was significant in rank tests, but loses its explanatory power in regressions. To the contrary, *bm* and *age* become significantly different from zero this time. The sign of *bm* is negative and significant at level 1 % in three regressions, consistent with my expectation that public investors know more about a high *bm* firm and do not react to the announcement a lot. However, the sign of *age* is significantly positive at level 5 %. The longer an issuer has been listed on the exchange, the higher the market reaction to the board announcement, evidence against the *Signaling Effect*. Thus I have

Table 5.5 Regression results on CAR_F

	1	2	3	4	5	6
Intercept	0.0224	0.1602	0.0105	0.0250*	0.1754	0.1571
	(1.46)	(1.49)	(0.60)	(1.87)	(1.41)	(1.30)
Δ*lsper*	0.0004					0.0006
	(0.54)					(0.65)
Δ*abscon*	−0.0149				−0.0083	
	(−0.92)				(−0.53)	
topten	0.006				−0.0029	−0.0031
	(0.06)				(−0.25)	(−0.28)
frac		0.0510			0.0689	0.0672
		(0.73)			(0.93)	(0.91)
size		−0.0142			−0.0165	−0.0149
		(−1.13)			(−1.16)	(−1.07)
bm		−0.0266			−0.0524	−0.0502
		(−0.44)			(−0.94)	(−0.90)
hitech		−0.0054			−0.0030	−0.0054
		(−0.46)			(−0.24)	(−0.43)
age		−0.0006			−0.0002	−0.0005
		(−0.46)			(−0.15)	(−0.35)
noin			0.0017		0.0020	0.0031
			(0.95)		(0.91)	(1.34)
liq				−0.1353	−0.2667	−0.2667
				(−0.43)	(−0.75)	(−0.75)
Δ*de*				−0.0031	−0.0029	−0.0033
				(−0.49)	(−0.41)	(−0.47)
roe	−0.0703	−0.0629	−0.0746	−0.08311	−0.0583	−0.0565
	(−1.26)	(−1.03)	(−1.37)	(−1.51)	(−0.92)	(−0.88)
leverage	0.0152	0.0258	0.0205	0.0250	0.0290	0.0279
	(0.59)	(0.85)	(0.80)	(0.65)	(0.88)	(0.85)
Year control	Yes	Yes	Yes	Yes	Yes	Yes
F statistic	0.67	0.91	1.14	0.72	0.74	0.75
Adj R^2	−0.0138	−0.0052	0.0035	−0.0092	−0.0266	−0.0254
Observations	505	505	505	505	505	505

This table shows OLS regression results of CAR_F on various independent variables. Δ*lsper* is the result of subtracting the controlling shareholder's percentage of holding before placement from the holding after. Holding data is collected via S_HOLDER_PCT. *frac* is calculated by shares offered in the offering and shares outstanding immediately after the offering. The former number is obtained from Wind's data screener "Primary Market", while the later using entry S_SHARE_TOTAL. I use S_FA_TA to obtain the value of *size*. I use S_FA_BPS to retrieve book value and S_VAL_MV to retrieve market value, so as to calculate *bm* by division. The value of *hitech* is determined manually by checking if an issuer belongs to the industries of Electronics, IT and Pharmaceutical and Biological Engineering. I use S_INFO_DLIST to retrieve the year when an issuer went public. The year of offering is available from data screener "Primary Market". Subtraction results in *age*. *noin* is obtained manually from *Detailed Statement*. *liq* is calculated as average trading volume of 30 trading days prior to board announcement over total shares outstanding before board announcement. Trading volume is retrieved using S_DQ_VOLUME. Δ*de* is the decrease in debt-to-equity ratio after the placement. Debt-to-equity ratio is obtained using S_FA_RATIODE. *roe* is return on common equity and obtained via S_FA_ROE. *leverage* is debt over the sum of debt and equity and can be calculated from debt-to-equity ratio

T-statistics are listed in the parentheses below coefficients

Significance levels of 1, 5 and 10 % are denoted by ***, ** and * respectively

found contradictory evidence for the *Signaling Effect* and, as in the case of testing on firm choice, cannot conclude that the reduction of information asymmetry has a positive effect on the market.

Table 5.5 shows no independent variable is significant in explaining cumulative abnormal return around final announcement. $\Delta lsper$ was significant in rank tests of the last section, but becomes insignificant in regression analysis. The coefficient of *topten* is not significantly different from zero either. Thus the market does not react to increased ownership concentration after the private placement, may it be from the largest shareholder or institutional investors.

All variables on information asymmetry are insignificant. This is different from the case of board announcement and I believe it due to information dispersion after the board has made the announcement. The market has incorporated all information regarding the private placement before final announcement. Although it appears hasty to conclude that the market does not react positively to new information that reduces information asymmetry, I find it fare to claim so, given the contrary evidence offered by the signs of *bm* and *age* in the regression for CAR_B. It is indeed hasty to conclude from the insignificance of *noin* that the market does not react positively to credible signals that the issuer has good prospects: Significance of *noin* may be damaged by improper information disclosure during the private placement process.

From coefficients of *liq* and Δde, I can also conclude that, opposite to Anderson et al. (2006), neither *Price Pressure Effect* nor *Wealth Transfer Effect* exists around a private placement's announcements.

References

Anderson HD, Rose LC, Cahan SF (2006) Differential shareholder wealth and volume effects surrounding private equity placements in New Zealand. Pacific-Basin Finance J 14:367–395

Hertzel M, Smith RL (1993) Market discounts and shareholder gains for placing equity privately. J Finance 48:459–485

Tan RSK, Chng PL, Tong YH (2002) Private placements and rights issues in Singapore. Pacific-Basin Finance J 10:29–54

Wruck KH (1989) Equity ownership concentration and firm value: evidence from private equity financings. J Financ Econ 23:3–28

Chapter 6
Long-Term Performance of Private Placements in China

Abstract In this chapter, I document positive long-run abnormal return of private offerings, evidence supportive of the under-reaction hypothesis. I then refer to findings in earlier chapters and argue that the largest shareholder does not deserve the excess discount in the placement. The largest shareholder can ask for a lower price than institutional investors' for longer locking period of private shares, but it does not, showing that liquidity is not a concern of it. It does not have to contribute capital to the issuer for under-subscription of shares, because no matter how uncertain firm value is, institutional investors are willing to dedicate enough proceeds. Thus information asymmetry is no problem for the largest shareholder either. Positive long-run abnormal return also does not justify the excess discount. I argue that the largest shareholder tunnels by excess discount, rational by itself but harmful to other shareholders.

Keywords Private Placement • PIPE • BHAR • Calender-time Approac • Fama-French Three Factors • Long-run Abnormal Return

Private placement in China has gained increasing traction on the stock market but not corresponding attention from financial economists. Research on the long-term performance of this equity refinancing method in China, since this method has been formally introduced to the market for only 5 years, is even scarcer. A long-term horizon is usually set to 5 years in event studies, such as Spiess and Affleck-Graves (1995), Loughran and Ritter (1997). In this chapter, considering data availability and meaningfulness of the calendar-time portfolio approach, I only analyze long-run performance up to two years after a private placement. This leads to the unfortunate fact that I have to reduce observations to those firms that completed private placements in 2007 and 2008.

P. Song, *Private Placement of Public Equity in China*, SpringerBriefs in Finance,
DOI: 10.1007/978-3-642-55093-5_6, © The Author(s) 2014

6.1 Research Agenda

I have documented positive announcement-period abnormal return for private placements in Chap. 5. Referring to the *Under-reaction Hypothesis* and the *Over-optimism Hypothesis* discussed in the literature review (see Sect. 2.5), I am interested in answering two sets of questions.

First, does the stock of a private shares issuer still perform better than its comparable benchmark long after the private placement? A positive answer to the question is evidence favorable to the *Under-reaction Hypothesis*. In this case, I would also like to know if the operating performance of the issuer is better than the control prior to the issue but deteriorates thereafter. If it does, I face the puzzle why investors under-react to the private placement announcement. If not, I can safely claim that the *Under-reaction Hypothesis* is supported.

Secondly, if the stock of a private shares issuer performs worse than its control in the long run, then over-optimism may be present when the placement is announced. In this scenario, if the operating performance of the issuer is better than the control prior to the issue but deteriorates thereafter, then the *Over-optimism Hypothesis* should not be rejected. Otherwise, I face the same problem as Hertzel et al. (2002) in not being able to justify the presence of over-optimism in their study using US data.

6.2 Methodologies and Data

6.2.1 Sample Selection

Private placement did not upgrade to a formal and well-regulated equity refinancing method in China's developing capital market until merely five years ago. To strike a balance between the number of sample points and the length of time horizon, I set the long-run time window to two years. As a result, the sample period of this study is reduced to years 2007 and 2008. The population is then all private placements completed in China's A-share market in these two years. I filter the population following three steps. First, observed firms that conducted private placements more than once and that also conducted SEO or rights offering between 2007 and 2011 are deleted. Second, observations in the financial services industry are deleted. Finally, I drop all observations with missing financial or market data. This process leaves me with a final sample of 247 observations. In 121 observations, the largest shareholder purchases shares in the private placement. Further still, in 42 of these 121 private offerings, the largest shareholder exchanges assets for shares, so a total of 79 transactions ($79 = 121 - 42$) in the sample are settled in cash. Table 6.1 exhibits the sample selection process.

Table 6.1 Process of sample construction

	Private placements
Original observations	254
Delete: multi-refinancing observations	4
Delete: financial firms	2
Delete: no share-holding data	1
Final sample	247
Shareholder participation	121
Purchase by assets	42
Purchase by cash	79

This table shows the data filtering process to reach the final sample I use in this chapter. Four observations whose issuers conduct multiple private placements, SEOs or rights offerings are deleted. I drop two observations in the financial services industry and one observation with missing share-holding data. For the final sample, I count the number of observations in which the controlling shareholder participates, purchases by assets and purchases by cash

6.2.2 Calculation of the Long-Run Abnormal Return

In order to avoid impacts from model misspecification, I employ two methods to calculate the long-run abnormal return of a private placement. Firstly I follow the approach suggested by Barber and Lyon (1997) and calculate BHAR (buy-and-hold abnormal return). Fama (1998), however, finds that the BHAR method results in multiplied estimation errors. Resorting to Mitchell and Stafford (2000), I utilize a second method *calendar-time portfolio* to measure long-term abnormal return.

The BHAR Method. For observation *i*, the stock's buy-and-hold abnormal return is calculated as

$$BHAR_i = BHR_i - BHR_{benchmark,i} = \prod_{t=1}^{T} \left(1 + R_{i,t}\right) - \prod_{t=1}^{T} \left(1 + R_{benchmark,i,t}\right) \tag{6.1}$$

In the equation above, $BHAR_i$ is the buy-and-hold abnormal return of the stock of observation i in holding period T. BHR_i and $BHR_{benchmark,i}$ are the buy-and-hold returns of stocks of company i's and its benchmark's in the holding period, respectively. $R_{i,t}$ and $R_{benchmark,i,t}$ are the monthly returns of i and its benchmark for month t, respectively.

The average buy-and-hold abnormal return of all observations is

$$BHAR = \frac{1}{N} \sum_{i=1}^{N} BHAR_i \tag{6.2}$$

in which N is number of observations in the sample.

For each firm i in my sample, I use size[1] (market capitalization) and BM (book-to-market ratio) as measures to determine its benchmark firm. First, from the set of all firms in China's A-share market, I choose five firms whose market capitalizations are closest to that of observation i's, with market capitalizations measured at end of the year before i's private placement. Secondly, from the five candidate benchmarks, I select the firm whose BM is closest to firm i's as its benchmark.

The Calendar-time Portfolio Method. I follow the method used in Fama and French (1993) and construct a three-factor model to test abnormal returns of sample firms. Specifically, I follow five steps described below.

Firstly, for year t, according to size and BM at the end of year $t-1$, I separate all stocks in China's A-share market into six portfolios. Specifically, all stocks are divided into two groups according to their size. The group of firms with market cap higher than the median is called the *Big Group*, while the left is called the *Small Group*. For both *Big* and *Small*, I further divide them into three groups according to the magnitude of BM: Firms ranking in the top 30 % belong to the *Growth Group*, firms in the last 30 % are called the *Value Group*, and these lying in the middle belong to the *Neutral Group*. Resultantly, I have six portfolios: *Small Growth*, *Small Neutral*, *Small Value*, *Big Growth*, *Big Neutral* and *Big Value*. Such portfolio formation is done three times: Yearly 2009–2011.

Secondly, I compute monthly returns for each portfolio. Weighted average is used,[2] and for month t, stock returns are weighted by market cap measured at the end of month $t-1$. It's noteworthy that total returns including reinvestment of dividends are used in calculations. For simplicity, I denote returns of each portfolio by the name of it.

Thirdly, I calculate *SMB* and *HML* for each month according to formulas

$$\begin{aligned} SMB = {} & \frac{1}{3}(Small\ Value + Small\ Neutral + Small\ Growth) \\ & - \frac{1}{3}(Big\ Value + Big\ Neutral + Big\ Growth) \end{aligned} \tag{6.3}$$

and

$$HML = \frac{1}{2}(Small\ Value + Big\ Value) - \frac{1}{2}(Small\ Growth + Big\ Growth) \tag{6.4}$$

Fourthly, I obtain excess market return by deducting the risk free rate (R_f) from market return (R_m). R_f at month t is calculated as the one-year savings rate published by PBOC (People's Bank of China) at t, divided by 12. R_m at month t is the weighted average of total returns of all shares in China's A-share market at month t, where weight is determined by market cap at month $t-1$.

The four steps above yield Fama-French three factors of China's A-share market for the 36 months of 2009, 2010 and 2011. Results are displayed in Table 6.2.

[1] Total assets value in Chaps. 3, 4 and 5 measures size. In this chapter, I use market cap as size.

[2] Equal weighting is also tried in my calculation, but does not make much difference.

Table 6.2 Fama-French three factors (China, 2009–2011)

Year	Month	R_f	R_m	SMB	HML	R_p
2009	1	0.0021	0.0822	0.1055	0.0433	0.3551
2009	2	0.0021	0.0507	0.0370	−0.0099	0.0304
2009	3	0.0021	0.1196	0.0605	−0.0086	0.1166
2009	4	0.0021	0.0287	−0.0046	−0.0149	0.0537
2009	5	0.0021	0.0626	0.0223	−0.0255	0.0478
2009	6	0.0021	0.0874	−0.0268	0.0138	−0.0094
2009	7	0.0021	0.1343	−0.0312	−0.0027	0.2067
2009	8	0.0021	−0.2981	−0.1062	−0.0023	0.1685
2009	9	0.0021	0.0358	0.0619	0.0109	0.2652
2009	10	0.0021	0.0777	0.0916	0.0660	0.1100
2009	11	0.0021	0.0387	0.1001	0.0101	0.0967
2009	12	0.0021	0.0130	0.0503	0.0443	0.2563
2010	1	0.0021	−0.0963	−0.0095	−0.0328	0.1624
2010	2	0.0021	0.0374	−0.1076	−0.0923	0.0192
2010	3	0.0021	0.0071	0.0588	0.0154	0.2403
2010	4	0.0021	−0.0965	−0.0451	−0.0055	0.1781
2010	5	0.0021	−0.1072	−0.0202	0.0469	−0.0948
2010	6	0.0021	−0.0776	−0.1007	−0.0177	−0.0222
2010	7	0.0021	0.1112	0.0966	0.0087	−0.1678
2010	8	0.0021	−0.0129	0.0499	0.0060	0.1985
2010	9	0.0021	0.0126	0.0667	−0.0051	−0.0809
2010	10	0.0021	0.0876	0.0752	0.0138	0.0632
2010	11	0.0023	−0.0830	0.0097	−0.0201	−0.2007
2010	12	0.0023	−0.0053	−0.0932	0.0130	−0.0177
2011	1	0.0023	−0.0222	0.0705	−0.0143	−0.0524
2011	2	0.0023	0.0382	0.0844	−0.0188	0.2164
2011	3	0.0025	0.0034	−0.0649	0.0148	0.0479
2011	4	0.0027	−0.0192	−0.0387	−0.0009	−0.0486
2011	5	0.0027	−0.0689	0.0253	−0.0184	0.2569
2011	6	0.0027	0.0069	0.0809	−0.0126	0.1080
2011	7	0.0029	−0.0215	−0.0711	−0.0259	−0.0466
2011	8	0.0029	−0.0493	−0.0123	−0.0099	0.1631
2011	9	0.0029	−0.0835	−0.0378	−0.0216	0.1080
2011	10	0.0029	0.0606	−0.0499	−0.0077	0.2384
2011	11	0.0029	−0.0578	−0.0326	−0.0069	−0.0780
2011	12	0.0029	−0.1005	−0.0373	−0.0006	−0.0632

This table lists China's Fama-French three factors in the 36 months of 2009–2011. R_f, the risk free rate, is calculated as one-year savings rate divided by 12. The one-year savings rate is obtained from PBOC's website. I use closing prices to calculate stock returns. Closing prices are obtained via S_DQ_CLOSE. Market value and book-to-market ratio are used to sort all stocks. The former is retrieved via S_VAL_MV and the latter S_FA_BPS and S_VAL_MV

Fifthly and finally, compliant with Loughran and Ritter (1997), Hertzel et al. (2002), I put China's Fama-French three factors into a calendar-time regression model formulated as

$$R_{pt} - R_{ft} = \alpha + \beta_m(R_{mt} - R_{ft}) + \beta_s SMB_t + \beta_h HML_t + \epsilon_t \quad (6.5)$$

in which R_{pt} is the value-weighted return at month t of all firms that have conducted private placements in the twenty four months before t. The intercept α measures average monthly abnormal return of the private placement portfolio.

6.3 Empirical Results

6.3.1 The BHAR Method

Table 6.3 presents average buy-and-hold returns (BHR) of my sample. I calculate BHR for four different holding periods: After private placement announcements, the 3-month, 6-month, 12-month and 24-month BHRs are 0.67, −2.31, −16.19 and 12.44 % respectively. The 3-month BHR is not significantly different from 0, the 6-month and 12-month BHRs are significantly negative, and the 24-month BHR is statistically positive. It appears that investments in privately placed shares experience negative return first, but then are able to reverse the downward trend and gain positive return. Similar BHRs of similar significance are documented for the subsample in which the largest shareholder participates in the private placement and the subsample in which the largest shareholder purchases shares with assets.

Table 6.4 takes benchmarks selected by size and BM into account and reports BHAR of private shares investments. Again, four holding periods are considered. As Panel A shows, after private placement announcements, the 3-month, 6-month, 12-month and 24-month BHARs are 9.99, 11.29, 22.12 and 32.42 % respectively, different from zero at significant levels of 1 % or lower. This is in sharp contrast with BHRs and tells that compared to investments in benchmarks, investing in private placements earns strictly positive returns in the long run. What's more, the return is increasing as time horizon goes longer. Long-run stock price behavior of subgroups within my sample is also considered. Panel A tells that BHARs of subsamples in which the largest shareholder purchases shares/does not purchase shares and these of subsamples in which the largest shareholder purchases shares with assets/cash are still positive and follow the same pattern of movement. The significance levels of BHARs for private placements in which the largest shareholder purchases by assets/cash are high. I conjecture this is due to the small number of observations in these subsamples.

Such long-run positive excess return is opposite to what Hertzel et al. (2002) find for the US case. Co-existence of positive short-run abnormal return and positive long-run abnormal return supports the *Under-reaction Hypothesis*: Favorable information is not fully impounded around the private placement announcement and the market continues with positive adjustments into the long end.

Panels B and C display results of difference analysis. Panel B shows that BHAR of the subsample with largest-shareholder participation is higher than that of the subsample in which only institutional investors purchase shares in all but the 12-month holding period. Two years after the private placement, the difference

Table 6.3 BHR of private placements

	N	3 Months		6 Months		12 Months		24 Months	
		BHR (%)	*p*-value	BHR (%)	*p*-value	BHR (%)	*p*-value	BHR (%)	*p*-value
Whole sample	247	0.67	(0.23)	−2.31	(0.00)	−16.19	(0.00)	12.44	(0.00)
No largest shareholder	126	0.62	(0.37)	−2.01	(0.00)	−14.78	(0.00)	13.85	(0.00)
Largest shareholder	121	0.69	(0.33)	−2.40	(0.00)	−18.39	(0.00)	12.78	(0.00)
Assets	42	0.71	(0.49)	−1.99	(0.09)	−16.23	(0.05)	12.83	(0.08)
Cash	79	0.65	(0.52)	−2.58	(0.05)	−44.03	(0.00)	12.60	(0.06)

This table shows buy-and-hold returns of private placements 3, 6, 12 and 24 months after placement. Starting date is 10 days after each placement. I use closing price to calculate stock return. Closing price is obtained via S_DQ_CLOSE

Table 6.4 BHAR of private placements

Hold period	N	3 Months		6 Months		12 Months		24 Months	
		BHAR (%)	*p*-value	BHAR (%)	*p*-value	BHAR (%)	*p*-value	BHAR (%)	*p*-value
Panel A: Overview									
Whole sample	247	9.99	(0.01)	11.29	(0.01)	22.12	(0.00)	32.42	(0.00)
No largest shareholder	126	7.25	(0.10)	7.42	(0.07)	28.31	(0.03)	30.98	(0.00)
Largest shareholder	121	14.14	(0.15)	15.61	(0.10)	15.25	(0.04)	34.03	(0.00)
Assets	42	15.59	(0.27)	32.35	(0.36)	11.85	(0.15)	32.02	(0.00)
Cash	79	12.27	(0.12)	−6.07	(0.11)	19.62	(0.06)	36.60	(0.00)
Panel B: BHAR difference between private placements participated by and not by the largest shareholder									
Largest shareholder –No largest shareholder		6.89	(0.245)	8.19	(0.389)	−13.06	(0.315)	3.05	(0.409)
Panel C: BHAR difference between private placements purchased by and not by assets									
Assets-Cash		3.32	(0.422)	38.42	(0.00)	−7.77	(0.407)	−4.58	(0.394)

This table shows buy-and-hold abnormal returns of private placements 3, 6, 12 and 24 months after placement. Starting date is ten days after each placement. I use closing price to calculate stock return. Closing price is obtained via S_DQ_CLOSE. In Panel B, I conduct mean-difference analysis for different subgroups of the sample. Market value and book-to-market ratio are used to select benchmarks for private placement issuers. The former is retrieved via S_VAL_MV, the latter S_FA_BPS and S_VAL_MV

Table 6.5 Calendar-time model

Variables	$R_p - R_f$	
	Coefficient	p-value
Intercept	0.0122	(0.027)
SMB	0.5699	(0.185)
HML	−1.2001	(0.055)
$R_m - R_f$	0.9345	(0.093)
Observations	36	
Adj R^2	0.1607	
F test	8.04	(0.097)
24-Month return	$(1 + \text{Intercept})^{24} - 1 = 0.3378$	

This table shows the result of regression of portfolio returns on risk free rate, market return, SMB and HML. Market cap is used to indicate size of a firm. I separate all stocks into two portfolios according to size and into three portfolios according to magnitude of book-to-market ratio. Market cap and BM ratio are retrieved by S_VAL_MV and S_FA_BPS respectively. I use closing price to calculate stock return. Closing price is obtained from S_DQ_CLOSE. Risk free rate is China's one-year savings rate divided by 12. The savings rate is obtained from PBOC's website

is as big as 3.05 %, but not statistically different from zero. Panel C shows that BHAR of the subsample in which the largest shareholder purchases shares with assets is smaller than that of the subsample in which the largest shareholder pays by cash in all but the 6-month holding period. Two years after the private placement, the difference is as big as −4.58 %, but not statistically significant either.

It would be intriguing if some independent variables could be found to hold explanatory power for the long-run abnormal return, as what Hertzel et al. (2002) hope but fail for the US case. I share the same bad luck with Hertzel et al. (2002) in not being able to find any useful independent variable for my sample, as I have failed to find significant explanatory variables for market reaction around final announcement. As discussed, dividing the sample by largest-shareholder participation or by purchase means of the largest shareholder does not yield significantly different BHARs across subsamples. I also divide the sample according to firm size, BM, discount level, announcement-period abnormal return, and all independent variables that appear in Chaps. 3, 4 and 5, but find resulting BHARs not significantly different for subsamples either. Due to limited space, I do not present the table of rank tests or regressions here. However, it is more than safe to claim that the BHAR method yields positive long-term abnormal returns, which reject the *Over-reaction Hypothesis* but cannot reject the *Under-reaction Hypothesis*.

6.3.2 The Calendar-Time Portfolio Method

Table 6.5 exhibits cumulative abnormal returns for private shares issuers obtained by applying Fama-French three factors. As the table shows, the monthly return of a value-weighted private placement portfolio in which all stocks went through private placements in the past 24 months is 1.22 %, larger than zero at 5 % significance level. The two-year return for the investment strategy of holding at month t a portfolio composed of stocks that did private placements between months $t - 24$ and $t - 1$ and rebalanced each month is 33.78 %, which equals $(1 + 1.22\ \%)^{24}$, very close to results in the BHAR method. The calendar-time portfolio method also points to significantly positive long-run abnormal return of an issuer after the private placement. Again, the *Over-optimism Hypothesis* is rejected, while the *Under-reaction Hypothesis* survives.

6.4 Operating Performance Before and After the Placement

Table 6.6 compares yearly operating performance of private placement firms and their benchmark firms in a five-year window, including two years before the placement, two years after the placement and the year that the placement takes place. Following Chou et al. (2009), I use four financial indicators: ROA (return on assets), ROE (return on equity), EPS (earnings per share), and CFFOPS (cash flow from operation per share).

As Table 6.6 shows, on average, the operating performance of a private shares issuer increases before the placement, reaches the maximum the year of placement, and then declines for the two years thereafter. Take ROA for example. The median ROA is 3.9 % two years prior to the placement year. It is 4.35 % one year later and reaches the maximum of 5.29 % in the placement year. One year past the placement, the median is 4.32. It decreases further to 2.58 the next year. The same pattern applies to other financial indicators of interest.

The operating performance of control firms follows the same inverted V pattern. I can conclude that such pattern is not unique to firms that conduct private placements in 2007 and 2008. Both sample firms and controls are subject to the same market influence. Specifically, the improvement of financial behavior at the beginning may due to completion of the stock-split reform, while subsequent deterioration may be attributable to the global financial meltdown. More in-depth investigation into the forces behind such inverted V pattern is beyond the scope of this book. The bottom line is there may be systematic risks imposed on both firms that conduct private placements and their benchmarks such that the same inverted V pattern is observed.

In order to eliminate systematic risks, I also do difference analysis in Table 6.6. The ROA of firms that conduct private placement is significantly higher than that of controls, with significance level 5 %, in all five years under investigation. It is the same for another two measures, ROE and EPS. What's a bit outstanding is CFFOPS. It is only in year -2 that CFFOPS of firms of private placement is significantly higher than that of controls. In the placement year, CFFOPS of the former is smaller, although statistically insignificant. After the placement, CFFOPS of the former becomes the larger one again, but not statistically significant. In summary, it is well established that firms that conduct private placements experience better operating performance both before and after the placement.

Table 6.6 Operating performance of private shares issuers

Year	−2	−1	0	1	2
ROA					
Sample firm (mean)	0.0372	0.0537	0.0759	0.0478	0.0365
Control firm (mean)	0.0253	0.0362	0.0445	0.0248	0.0230
Difference (sample-control)	0.0119	0.0175	0.0314	0.0230	0.0135
p-value	(0.0353)	(0.001)	(0.008)	(0.001)	(0.008)
Wilcoxon z value	3.340	3.427	3.693	3.000	2.510
ROE					
Sample firm (mean)	0.0372	0.0537	0.0759	0.0478	0.0365
Control firm (mean)	0.0253	0.0362	0.0445	0.0248	0.0230
Difference (sample-control)	0.0119	0.0175	0.0314	0.0230	0.0135
p-value	(0.0353)	(0.001)	(0.008)	(0.001)	(0.008)
Wilcoxon z value	3.340	3.427	3.693	3.000	2.510
EPS					
Sample firm (mean)	0.0372	0.0537	0.0759	0.0478	0.0365
Control firm (mean)	0.0253	0.0362	0.0445	0.0248	0.0230
Difference (sample-control)	0.0119	0.0175	0.0314	0.0230	0.0135
p-value	(0.0353)	(0.001)	(0.008)	(0.001)	(0.008)
Wilcoxon z value	3.340	3.427	3.693	3.000	2.510
CFFOPS					
Sample firm (mean)	0.0372	0.0537	0.0759	0.0478	0.0365
Control firm (mean)	0.0253	0.0362	0.0445	0.0248	0.0230
Difference (sample-control)	0.0119	0.0175	0.0314	0.0230	0.0135
p-value	(0.0353)	(0.001)	(0.008)	(0.001)	(0.008)
Wilcoxon z value	3.340	3.427	3.693	3.000	2.510

This table shows private shares issuers' operating performance for 5 years around the placement. I use S_FA_ROA, S_FA_ROE, S_FA_EPS, and S_FA_CFFOPS to retrieve data on ROA, ROE, EPS and CFFOPS respectively. Mean-difference analysis is also conducted

Two points are worth mentioning here. First, my finding is different from Hertzel et al. (2002) who document that the financial behavior of private placement firms is worse than that of controls after the placement in the US. Second, earlier I claim that the *Over-optimism Hypothesis* does not hold in China, now I can further conclude that although the financial strength of firms that place shares privately is stronger than that of control firms prior to the placement, investors in China are not necessarily over-optimistic about firm prospect. This is in contrast to Loughran and Ritter (1997)'s claim that investors facing recent good financial indicators act over-optimistically. It seems that investors in China are more conservative than these in the US. However, whether this is the case is beyond the scope of this book.

I divide the sample into subsamples and look into the operating performance of subsamples in Table 6.7. Firstly, I consider private placements in which the issuer's largest shareholder purchases shares and these in which only institutional investors participate. Two years prior to the placement, ROA and ROE of the former subsample are smaller than these of the latter group, significantly at 10 % level. Differences of the two indicators become insignificant in the placement year.

Table 6.7 Operating performances across private shares issuers

Year	−2	−1	0	1	2
Panel A: Operating performance across private placements participated by and not by the largest shareholder					
ROA					
Largest shareholder (mean)	0.0372	0.0537	0.0759	0.0478	0.0365
No largest shareholder (mean)	0.0253	0.0362	0.0445	0.0248	0.0230
Difference (LS-NLS)	0.0119	0.0175	0.0314	0.0230	0.0135
p-value	(0.0353)	(0.001)	(0.008)	(0.001)	(0.008)
Wilcoxon z value	3.340	3.427	3.693	3.000	2.510
ROE					
Largest shareholder (mean)	0.0372	0.0537	0.0759	0.0478	0.0365
No largest shareholder (mean)	0.0253	0.0362	0.0445	0.0248	0.0230
Difference (LS-NLS)	0.0119	0.0175	0.0314	0.0230	0.0135
p-value	(0.0353)	(0.001)	(0.008)	(0.001)	(0.008)
Wilcoxon z value	3.340	3.427	3.693	3.000	2.510
EPS					
Largest shareholder (mean)	0.0372	0.0537	0.0759	0.0478	0.0365
No largest shareholder (mean)	0.0253	0.0362	0.0445	0.0248	0.0230
Difference (LS-NLS)	0.0119	0.0175	0.0314	0.0230	0.0135
p-value	(0.0353)	(0.001)	(0.008)	(0.001)	(0.008)
Wilcoxon z value	3.340	3.427	3.693	3.000	2.510
CFFOPS					
Largest shareholder (mean)	0.0372	0.0537	0.0759	0.0478	0.0365
No largest shareholder (mean)	0.0253	0.0362	0.0445	0.0248	0.0230
Difference (LS-NLS)	0.0119	0.0175	0.0314	0.0230	0.0135
p-value	(0.0353)	(0.001)	(0.008)	(0.001)	(0.008)
Wilcoxon z value	3.340	3.427	3.693	3.000	2.510
Panel B: Operating performance across private placements purchased by and not by assets					
ROA					
Assets (mean)	0.0372	0.0537	0.0759	0.0478	0.0365
Cash (mean)	0.0253	0.0362	0.0445	0.0248	0.0230
Difference (assets–cash)	0.0119	0.0175	0.0314	0.0230	0.0135
p-value	(0.0353)	(0.001)	(0.008)	(0.001)	(0.008)
Wilcoxon z value	3.340	3.427	3.693	3.000	2.510
ROE					
Assets (mean)	0.0372	0.0537	0.0759	0.0478	0.0365
Cash (mean)	0.0253	0.0362	0.0445	0.0248	0.0230
Difference (assets–cash)	0.0119	0.0175	0.0314	0.0230	0.0135
p-value	(0.0353)	(0.001)	(0.008)	(0.001)	(0.008)
Wilcoxon z value	3.340	3.427	3.693	3.000	2.510
EPS					
Assets (mean)	0.0372	0.0537	0.0759	0.0478	0.0365
Cash (mean)	0.0253	0.0362	0.0445	0.0248	0.0230
Difference (assets–cash)	0.0119	0.0175	0.0314	0.0230	0.0135
p-value	(0.0353)	(0.001)	(0.008)	(0.001)	(0.008)
Wilcoxon z value	3.340	3.427	3.693	3.000	2.510
CFFOPS					

(continued)

Table 6.7 (continued)

Year	−2	−1	0	1	2
Assets (mean)	0.0372	0.0537	0.0759	0.0478	0.0365
Cash (mean)	0.0253	0.0362	0.0445	0.0248	0.0230
Difference (assets–cash)	0.0119	0.0175	0.0314	0.0230	0.0135
p-value	(0.0353)	(0.001)	(0.008)	(0.001)	(0.008)
Wilcoxon z value	3.340	3.427	3.693	3.000	2.510

This table shows private shares issuers' operating performance for 5 years around the placement. I use S_FA_ROA, S_FA_ROE, S_FA_EPS, and S_FA_CFFOPS to retrieve data on ROA, ROE, EPS and CFFOPS respectively. Mean-difference analysis is also conducted

However, the former subsample gets significantly higher ROA and ROE again after the placement, at significance level 10 %. EPS and CFFOPS are significantly higher for the former group in the placement year, but become lower later, albeit insignificantly. This points to the fact that although the largest shareholder may purchase shares in a private placement, it does not make noticeable contribution to the firm's financial strength after the placement.

Secondly, I make comparisons between private placements in which the largest shareholder buys shares with assets and these in which the largest shareholder pays by cash. As Table 6.7 indicates, the former subsample has lower ROA, ROE and EPS two years prior to the placement. The difference is significant at level 10 % for ROA and ROE. After the placement, however, all three measures for the former group become larger and differences are at significance level 5 %. Although I find no noticeable discrepancies for CFFOPS of the two subsamples, it is safe to claim there is evidence that private placements in which the largest shareholder injects assets into the issuer are associated with improved post-placement operating performance.

6.4.1 Robustness Test

In this chapter, I make sure that my results are robust with efforts along two lines. First, to better capture the long-run stock return, I calculate CARs (cumulative abnormal returns, as discussed in Chap. 5) of the sample against control firms, in addition to BHARs and Fama-French three factors. I do this exercise albeit CAR is more popular in studies focusing on the announcement period. There is no significant difference between results from the CAR method and the BHAR method. This offers further evidence that long-run abnormal return is significantly positive for private-placement firms in China.

Second, in studying operating performance within the five-year window, besides using control firms (benchmarks), I also compare financial indicators of sample firms with medians of corresponding industries and obtain similar conclusions. In this case, medians of ROA, ROE, EPS and CFFOPS of all firms in a private-placement firm's industry are considered benchmarks. I do not list all results thanks to limited space.

References

Barber BM, Lyon JD (1997) Detecting abnormal operating performance: the empirical power and specification of test statistics. J Financ Econ 41:359–399

Chou DW, Gombola M, Liu FY (2009) Long-run underperformance following private equity placements: The role of growth opportunities. Q Rev Econ Finan 49:1113–1128

Fama E (1998) Market efficiency, long-term returns, and behavioral finance. J Financ Econ 49:283–306

Fama E, French KR (1993) Common risk factors in the returns on stocks and bonds. J Financ Econ 33:3–56

Hertzel M, Lemmon M, Linck JS, Rees L (2002) Long-run performance following private placements of equity. J Finan 57:2595–2617

Loughran T, Ritter J (1997) The operating performance of firms conducting seasoned equity offerings. J Finan 52:1823–1850

Mitchell ML, Stafford E (2000) Managerial decisions and long-term stock price performance. CRSP working paper no. 453, CRSP

Spiess DK, Affleck-Graves J (1995) Underperformance in long-run stock returns following seasoned equity offerings. J Financ Econ 38:243–267

Chapter 7
Conclusion: From the Perspective of Interest Parties

Abstract This chapter concludes the book and shows how various interest parties are influenced by a private placement in China.

Keywords Private Placement • PIPE • Discount • Abnormal Return • Market Reaction • Tunneling

The Market. Public investors react a positive 4.30 % to the board announcement and slightly less to the final announcement of a placement. Regression analysis shows the market does not respond to either the controlling shareholder's increased holdings or the fact that there are institutional investors becoming substantial blockholders. There is mixed evidence whether the reduction of information asymmetry on firm value induces positive market reaction. The claim that more credible information leads to higher market reaction cannot be supported, but this may due to information disclosure from insiders to the market before the final announcement.

The Issuer. Facing the choice between private placement and SEO as feasible means of refinancing, a listed firm whose controlling shareholder is a state-owned entity is more likely to choose private placement than its counterpart whose controlling shareholder is private. This may be due to CSRC's attitude that is more favorable to state-owned entities. Private placement is also preferred to SEO by firms wanting to establish business connections with investors via equity refinancing, since it is easier for the investor to get targeted amount of shares by the former method. I find mixed evidence whether a more information asymmetric firm is more likely to use private placement as a solution to underinvestment.

Existing Small Shareholders of the Issuer. Besides positive short-run abnormal returns around announcements of the placement, in the long run, small stock holders of private shares issuers enjoy a 24-month return of 12.44 %, higher by 32.42 % than investing in benchmark firms. This does not mean small shareholders' interests are well protected from being encroached. In a private placement where the controlling shareholder purchases shares, the discount is higher by 34.81 % than that of a private placement in which institutional investors are the

P. Song, *Private Placement of Public Equity in China*, SpringerBriefs in Finance, DOI: 10.1007/978-3-642-55093-5_7,

only purchaser. As I have argued, this is a way of tunneling wealth from small shareholders to the controlling shareholder. Net benefit to small shareholders, however, is difficult to measure and beyond the scope of this study.

Institutional Investors. In a private placement where institutional investors are the only purchaser, they buy shares at a discount of 8.80 %. If the largest shareholder joins them in the offering, they enjoy an extra discount of 34.81 %. Whether in the later case these two types of investors are colluding is beyond scope of this book. Besides the discount, participating institutional investors on average receive a 24-month return of 12.44 %, higher by 32.42 % than investing in private shares issuers' benchmark firms, a lucrative investment strategy by any standard. Whether this pattern of return will continue is left for future study.

The Controlling Shareholder. Given that a listed firm has decided to do a private placement, its largest shareholder does not take holdings dilution into account when making the decision whether to purchase shares or not. What's more, the largest shareholder does not have to worry about information asymmetry between firm insiders and investors: Investors cannot be more willing to contribute capital to the issuer. The largest shareholder enjoys an extra discount of 34.81 % in offering price, and also a 12.44 % 24-month abnormal return. In this sense, the controlling shareholder is the biggest winner of this private placement game. I argue that it does not deserve the excess discount. Information asymmetry has no explanatory power. In the long run, the issuer's stock performs better than the benchmark. Conclusively, there is no reason but tunneling that explains the excess discount.

MIX
Papier aus verantwortungsvollen Quellen
Paper from responsible sources
FSC® C105338

If you have any concerns about our products,
you can contact us on
ProductSafety@springernature.com

In case Publisher is established outside the EU,
the EU authorized representative is:
Springer Nature Customer Service Center GmbH
Europaplatz 3, 69115 Heidelberg, Germany

Printed by Libri Plureos GmbH
in Hamburg, Germany